ALABAMA
SHOWDOWN

ALSO BY GEOFFREY NORMAN

Midnight Water
The Orvis Book of Upland Bird Shooting
The Ultimate Fishing Book

ALABAMA SHOWDOWN

THE
FOOTBALL RIVALRY
BETWEEN
AUBURN AND ALABAMA

GEOFFREY NORMAN

HENRY HOLT AND COMPANY / NEW YORK

Published by Henry Holt and Company, Inc.
521 Fifth Avenue, New York, New York 10175.
Published simultaneously in Canada.

Library of Congress Cataloging in Publication Data
Norman, Geoffrey.
Alabama showdown.
1. Auburn University—Football—History.
2. University of Alabama—Football—History.   I. Title.
GV958.A92N67   1987   796.332'72   86-9984
ISBN 0-8050-0081-X

First Edition

Designed by Jeffrey L. Ward
Printed in the United States of America
1 3 5 7 9 10 8 6 4 2

Portions of this book originally appeared
in *Southern Magazine*.

ISBN 0-8050-0081-X

for
Susan S. Norman,
a real Alabama lady

Contents

Introduction:
Into the Blood

The middle of November is a turning time in Alabama. Always has been and always will be. That much will endure even when everything else has changed.

The signs are there. You can see it in the few remaining cotton fields shot through with bright white blossoms ready to be picked and ginned. Or in the woods that are going from green to brown, where the deer are marking territory and fighting each other to defend it. In the old days, November was when people would be putting down the plow and picking up the gun.

Those days are gone—they grow cotton in Arizona now—but the rhythms survive. One hundred and twenty years after the Civil War; fifty years after the Great Depression; thirty years after the civil rights movement (which got started with a bus boycott in Montgomery); and ten years after the advent of the Sun Belt and the New South . . . after all of that, much of Alabama *looks* like most of every other place. You see four-lane highways, high-rise buildings, and franchise restaurants. People do aerobics, drive German

cars, and own condominiums at the beach. They get HBO
from the cable or the dish. They go to Europe. Drink wine.
Eat sushi. Read the *Wall Street Journal*.

But though Alabama looks like every other place (lots
of Alabama, but not *all* of it . . . yet), in mid-November it
feels like no other place on earth. The old rhythms are still
there, under the surface of things. In the blood, maybe.
Beneath all the superficial changes, something fundamental survives. And this year, during the last two weeks of
November, it comes boiling up to the surface and finds its
voice in the language of football.

The actual football season begins in early September and
for two and a half months fans follow the University of
Alabama and Auburn University with rapt and rising attention. For Alabama this season, it has been a better year
than almost anyone expected, though this does not mean
it has been good enough. For Auburn, the school ranked
eighth in the country with a star player regarded as a
favorite to win the Heisman trophy, perhaps the most prestigious individual honor in all of sport, it has been a disappointing year.

But . . . all that is in the past. The season has come down
to one game for both schools—the game they play against
each other. They will play it on the last day of November
in 1985. There will be two weeks for the teams to prepare
for this game; two weeks of increasingly feverish anticipation for the fans and the newspapers. Two weeks for the
state to settle into a fine hysteria.

Everybody cares about the game. Everybody is either
an Auburn fan or an Alabama fan. There is nobody an
Auburn fan wants to beat more than Alabama. Nobody an
Alabama fan hates losing to more than Auburn.

You can salvage a whole season of pride in this game.
Or ruin an otherwise unblemished year.

For two weeks, then, Alabama might look like every
other place but feels like a place all its own. Everybody
feels it. Fans, players, coaches. Even a visitor from the
North. It starts Saturday afternoon. For Alabama, when

it has gotten by Southern Mississippi in a damp and somewhat lackluster performance in Tuscaloosa. For Auburn, after a decisive, satisfying win over Georgia, in Athens, that leaves fans crying "WAAAAAAAAAAR EAGLE!" into the night and shouting "Bring on Bama! Bring on Bama!"

At that moment, two weeks seems like a long time to wait.

ALABAMA
SHOWDOWN

1

Sunday
with the Coach

On Sunday morning Ray Perkins was up early, as usual. In Alabama, football coaches rise with the farmers. Bear Bryant would customarily arrive at his office by six, sometimes earlier. They still like to tell the story of how he called Auburn one morning and reached the athletic department where someone told him that nobody had come in to work yet. It was seven A.M. "What's the matter," Bryant said in that profound voice of his, "don't you Auburn people take your football seriously?"

Ray Perkins, whose lot it has been to follow Bryant at Alabama, works as long and as hard as Bryant ever did. During the season, he is at his office by five most mornings. It is often close to midnight when he leaves.

But this morning, he is not going to the office until later. First he must drive out McFarland Boulevard, past the motels where the signs still read "Go Tide, Beat Southern," and the guests are still sleeping off the celebrations that followed yesterday's game, and turn off on Jug Factory Road, which winds past some unpainted shacks and a sign

1

that points to "Dreamland," where you go for Tuscaloosa's best bar-b-que, to a small television studio where he pulls in and parks the gun gray Lincoln, which is given to him as a courtesy by a local dealer. He gets a new one every year. The dealer considers it an honor.

Ray Perkins is the head football coach of the University of Alabama and, as such, one of the three most visible and important men in the state. The other two are Pat Dye, the head coach of Auburn, and George Wallace. In fact, Ray Perkins may be even more controversial than the old fire-breathing segregationist. Everyone in Alabama has an opinion or a theory about Perkins and would be only too happy to share it with you. After all these years, Wallace is just Wallace.

The sun is coming up as Perkins walks across the parking lot to the door of the red brick building. Roosters are crowing in bare-earth yards where they scratch and strut during the day. A dog barks and a lone owl hoots once in reply.

There is dew on the ground and the air feels wet. It is still warm, even for Alabama, in mid-November. The live oaks and the dogwoods are still green. Perkins wears a sport jacket, no overcoat.

He steps into a room where several men are sitting around a table drinking coffee and waiting for him. One of the men is Gus Hergert, the producer of the television show Perkins is here to tape. The other men are technicians, except for Dennis Homan, who is Perkins's co-host on the television show and was his teammate twenty years ago. They were both All-American receivers for Alabama on what Bear Bryant once called his greatest team.

"Morning," Perkins says, shaking hands all around.

"Good game, Coach," Hergert says.

"Thank you," Perkins replies. "I thought so too."

Ray Perkins is forty-four years old. He does not look it, but neither does he look like someone who has devoted much time to looking young. He looks like the sort of man who would consider such an effort a waste of time, frivolous. And Ray Perkins, by reputation and by first impression, is not a man who tolerates frivolity.

He is a little over six feet. Probably a little under two hundred pounds. He has straight brown hair, fashionably styled but going thin to bald in back, and a narrow, angular face dominated by a pair of level, penetrating, pale blue eyes that writers inevitably call "steely."

Perkins has a way of looking straight into the eyes of anyone he is talking to that most people find unnerving. This is what writers have called his "gunfighter stare." He combines it with long silences following, say, a question from a reporter. About the silence, with the stare, a sportswriter once said, "You wonder whether he's going to answer your question, ignore it, or call you a dumb sumbitch and beat the living hell out of you."

This morning, though his team won yesterday and he has two weeks to prepare for his next game, Perkins is quick to get down to business. He lets Hergert dab a little makeup over a shaving cut, but he is plainly impatient.

He and Homan take their places in two chairs facing a camera. There is no desk or platform in front of them. They could be sitting, stranded, at an airport.

The music comes up and the cameras roll.

The coach's television show is part of the recipe of Southern football, a small but necessary ingredient, like filé to gumbo. Without the TV show, there would still be football, but it wouldn't be quite so savory.

Nobody is really sure just where or when the coach's show got its start, but it is a historical fact that, like so much else in football, it was refined, perfected, and permanently established by Paul W. Bryant. He turned the coach's show into a minor regional art form that became as much a part of Sunday in the South as racing stock cars and preaching the Word.

The format is simplicity itself. The coach and a friendly interviewer sit in some variation of the basic TV studio set and talk about yesterday's game. Some of the time, the coach and his interviewer are on camera, but most of the time the audience is watching filmed highlights of the game. Coach is there to say his piece about the way the team played and to create the illusion of something intimate going on here. Viewers, if they suspend disbelief enough, can imagine themselves sitting with the coach and grading film the way he does with his assistants. It would be like reading *Finnegans Wake* with the world's foremost Joyce scholar. Or, more aptly, like hunting turkeys with Ben Rogers Lee or fishing for bass with Tom Mann.

Of course, no coach, not even Bryant, is secure enough to say on camera, to a mass audience, what he would say in private to his assistants. But it was Bryant's genius to make the viewers believe that this was the case, to perform on his show in a fashion that couldn't have been anything, viewers thought, but spontaneous and authentic.

Bryant had a big head full of thick bones and he would have looked like an ignorant son of the soil, except that he was handsome enough to have been offered a screen test once. As he aged and worked himself to exhaustion, his big handsome face developed deep lines and wrinkles that looked more like folds. When he tried for solemnity, he looked like a country preacher drenched in woe.

"Well," he would say as he looked into the camera, "we managed to beat Tennessee yesterday, in spite of a bad job of coaching on my part. We were poorly prepared and we'd done a bad job of scouting. But the players went out there and played the way they had to and I just can't tell you how proud I am of them. I promised them after the game that I would never let them down like that again. They are a wonderful bunch of young men and I'm just proud as I can be of them."

After that, the co-host would be reduced to something like, "Well, Coach, that's mighty fine. Now what do you say we look at the film."

So the film would roll and Bryant might say, as the first play was made, "That's little old Drew Jones, there, making the tackle on that one. Drew comes from down around Eufala. His daddy's got a bait and tackle store down there and everytime I'm in the area, I stop by and we talk fishing. I believe Drew's daddy knows as much about fishing as anyone in the state and his mama makes a fine pecan pie.

I've stopped over there many a time to visit. They were in the stands yesterday, watching Drew, and I'm sure they were real proud of him."

Meanwhile, on film, three or four plays would have been run and the ball might have turned over while Bryant was still talking about some boy's daddy and mama and how he can still remember the last time he was by their place, eating pecan pie.

"We've got an interception coming up here I think, Coach."

"Yeah. Sudden changes [Bryant's phrase for turnovers], those'll get you every time. We work on them a lot because we know there'll be a couple of those every game. Not being ready for those sudden changes, Charley, that's how you lose football games."

"That's right, Coach."

By now, the action would be four or five plays into the drive following the turnover.

"Now here's what I'm talking about with poor coaching, Charley," Bryant would say as one of the opposing backs ran a punt back for a long gain, breaking two or three tackles. "We should have known about that little punt returner of theirs. Should have known about his speed and those moves. *Look at those moves.* But we did a poor job of scouting and a poor job of preparation and our boys just weren't ready. So they break a couple on us and almost run one back all the way. It was just a case of poor coaching."

At this point the half would come to a close and Bryant would say some effusive things about the band as it marched onto the field to perform. Then it would be time for a commercial.

The commercial would consist of a Bryant testimonial for Coca-Cola and Golden Flake potato chips. Bryant would talk about the wonderful taste of Coca-Cola and how there just wasn't anything that could beat it when you had a real thirst, the kind that working hard gave you. Then he would tilt up a bottle of Coca-Cola and gulp down a few swallows. And all over the state people would wonder if he had something more than just Coca-Cola in that bottle to get him through the Sunday morning filming of that TV show. It was never any secret that Bryant liked whiskey.

Then he would take a few handfuls of potato chips and put them in his mouth and chew them like a horse working on hay. You could hear the crunch of those potato chips over the studio microphones and it sounded like someone grinding glass. Bryant would talk about how Golden Flake potato chips were just about the best-tasting things you could put in your mouth, especially if you washed them down with a little Coca-Cola.

Bryant did testimonials the same way he did everything else. Hard. Some of his more sophisticated defenders said you could see him winking when he did them, they were so theatrical. It was as if he were saying, *Now you know I don't have to do this, it's just for the money, and I don't even really need that.* Others who knew him well said he tried just as hard to sell potato chips and soft drinks as he did to win football games, and that he never looked on an opportunity to earn money any way but absolutely seriously. It was a measure of Bryant's size and complexity that you could believe both things about him at the same time. Probably he could too.

After the half-time commercial, the film would roll again and Bryant would start talking about the boy who just made that catch and how his daddy up in Decatur would be so proud of him. His daddy runs a little sawmill, his mama cooks the best pork chops; he's a little boy, but he plays his heart out and when you look at the films you'll be looking at his number on almost every play . . . and so on, as the game rolled on.

Then, in the middle of his meandering monologue, just as it was on the verge of going from entertaining to boring, the film would show a hard tackle and Bryant would shout into his microphone, "Merciful heavens, did you see *that*? What a tackle! That's the way you like to see them hitting out there. Who made that tackle?"

"I don't know, Coach."

"Well, we'll find out when the coaches study the film. When somebody can hit that hard, I want to know who it is. Looked like Lee Roy Jordan out there, but Lee Roy's been graduated for three years."

By now, the game would be running down and so would Bryant. He would be uttering the platitudes of coaching the way a preacher falls back on the beatitudes of scripture: "Clean, hard-fought game, nobody has anything to be ashamed of . . . we got some breaks and we took advantage of them . . . held on to the ball and the other team didn't . . . played hard and stayed alert and that's how you win football games . . . proud of our defense, but our offense did a real good job too. . . ."

And so on, until the last sip of Coca-Cola and the last mouthful of potato chips and the "Goodbye until next week." The people watching loved it. This was as close as they would ever get, most of them, to sitting in the same room with the man they most admired in the world. They loved him for being sincere or, if they were subtle, for sincerely *trying* to be sincere. Either way, you could not watch the show without being charmed and feeling that you were seeing at least a part of Paul Bryant just as he was.

Bryant's show became an institution. Professional television producers hated it and were embarrassed by it. They thought it played to, and showed, the worst side of the South. But it was hugely popular, which, of course, meant that it spawned imitators. Today, virtually every coach of a major football power has his own highlights show. It is a good way for the football program to get more exposure and it is a good way for a coach to make more money.

Each show has its own distinctive style. No doubt most of the show's style is a reflection of the coach's personality. They are all produced by professionals who have their own ideas, but head football coaches are used to getting things done their way.

The early Bryant shows were done in black and white, in studio settings that were positively barren by today's standards. Today production values are up. One coach, Bobby Bowden of Florida State, is big on show business.

The lead-in is done by Burt Reynolds, who once played at Florida State. Vince Dooley, on the other hand, is staid and formal enough on his show that he could be in the Senate, which is where he considered going last summer for a few tense weeks in the Georgia sports pages.

Ray Perkins's show is without gimmicks. It opens today with credits and a tape of the Alabama fight song. Then the camera focuses on Homan, who describes yesterday's win over Southern Mississippi and then introduces Perkins, who looks into the camera and forces a smile. He calls the game "a great win," and says he is proud of the way his team came from behind in the fourth quarter. As he talks, film highlights of the game begin to roll.

Perkins's narration is basic American Footballese.

"They run the *option* as well as any team we've played. They can be real dangerous with that *option*."

"Mike Shula did a good job, Dennis. He played a *smart* football game."

"Cornelius Bennett is what I call an *impact* player."

"Right here, in this drive, we do pretty much what we have to do to get the job done."

And so forth. Perkins provides a sound, serviceable voice-over for the action on camera. He stays with the plays and he has learned, according to Hergert, to keep his remarks short and to the point so that his descriptions of one play will not run over into the next several. His voice is a little thin and nasal, but he has taught himself inflection. He also studies the game statistics so that while he is describing a particular defensive play he can mention that his team allowed so many yards rushing and so many passing. In other words, he comes prepared.

The closest this morning's show comes to genuine spontaneity is when an Alabama receiver drops a pass that would have been a certain touchdown.

"Ahhh," Homan groans, "he was looking to score before he caught the ball."

"Yeah, I really felt bad for him," Perkins says, "but he'll get other chances and I know he won't drop them."

"Well, you and I have dropped one or two, haven't we, Coach."

"In practice . . ."

"No, *I've* dropped 'em in ball games."

It is a nice moment and everyone in the control room smiles.

To close the show, Homan asks Perkins a question about the game that will be played in two weeks against Auburn. Perkins says, "They've got a fine football team and it will be a fine game. We'll have to play our best game of the year to win."

The music comes up and the show closes with the credits running over the Alabama fight song. Perkins takes off his microphone, says a few words to Homan, and leaves. He has a busy day and a busy two weeks ahead of him getting ready for Auburn.

Dennis Homan stays behind a few minutes and talks to the technicians while he has another cup of coffee. He is asked about Perkins, who is one of those people who seem always a little mysterious and unknowable. "Tell me what he's *really* like," people will ask someone who might know.

"You know, Ray was probably the most intense player on those '65 and '66 teams," Homan says. "And we had some pretty intense people. A lot of them just lived football. But Ray was probably more that way than anybody. He used to watch film all the time. When we were on the road, he'd get up early so he could watch film before the game. You hear about players doing that in the pros, but you don't see it much in college."

"Yeah, but you know what's funny. He's easier to work with after a loss," Hergert says. "After the Tennessee game, he came in here and said, 'Can we get on with this? I'm not in a very good mood this morning and I got a lot of things to do.' We rolled the tape and he was out of here in thirty-seven minutes. When he wins, he doesn't mind doing three or four takes of something. And he'll screw around with the set and ask me a lot of questions about this and that. This morning was a little different . . . but he's got Auburn to think about."

"Well, I like to see it," Homan says. "I like to see us winning and I like to see him relaxing. It would be nice if the people who get on him so hard could see him that way."

"All they ever see is those eyes."

"Seems like he's smiled, oh, two or three times now this season," one of the technicians says.

"That's what winning will do for you."

"He'll really be smiling if he beats Auburn."

"That'll do it for sure," Homan says. "If he wins that one, then it's a great season."

"And if he loses it?"

"It's not a great season," Homan says. "Simple as that."

The tape is put in a can and sent on to Birmingham for satellite feed. It will be shown throughout the state on dozens of stations at all hours of the day and night.

People will watch the show. None of them will be offended or amused or touched by it, though a lot of viewers will wish, as they watch this slick, professional production, that the Bear were still around, doing the old black and white show, swilling down Coca-Cola, eating potato chips, and saying "Merciful heavens" when one of his boys made a hard tackle. Nothing wrong with this show, they will think. But somehow, it just ain't the same.

Ray Perkins once said he was only following Bryant, he was not "replacing" him. He couldn't replace him and he wouldn't even try. Pat Dye, however, never said he wouldn't try, and some days he seemed to be trying very hard. People in Alabama who missed Bryant and wanted to watch something on television that brought back warm memories of him could watch Dye's show, which ran all across the state, just like "The Ray Perkins Show."

Dye is the head coach of Auburn University. His team will be playing Perkins's team in two weeks in the most important football game of the year.

This morning Dye is congratulating his team on its fine victory over Georgia the day before. The camera is in the locker room and Dye is talking to his players. "Men, I'm proud of you. Mighty proud," he says, his voice full of feeling, with cadences that powerfully recall Bryant. "You beat a fine football team today. Beat 'em straight up. Didn't get no lucky breaks or no favors from anyone. You beat 'em by playing football like I know you can play it. And I'll tell you something. If you play football like that in two weeks' time, then you're going to win in Birmingham."

The team cheers and then sings the Auburn fight song, every man joining in and clapping to provide the rhythm. Even on the television screen, their joy is contagious. You watch and want to clap and sing with them. If you played football, you think, you'd want to play for Pat Dye.

This lead-in to the show is a wonderful moment of television for any college football fan, no matter what loyalty. The camera goes into the dressing room with the team right after the final gun so the viewer sees the players coming through the door, wet, tired, happy, and occasionally bloody. Yelling and smiling and pounding on each other, full of the feeling of victory and absolutely oblivious to the camera.

Going into the locker room with the camera was Dye's idea. He told his co-host, Phil Snow, that they were "going to have to coach the alumni as well as the players."

"When he came to Auburn," Snow says, "Pat took over a losing team. This was '81. Alabama had won a national championship in '79 and was talking about another. Auburn wasn't going anywhere for a while.

"He figured if we showed the players in the locker room, got the idea across that even though we didn't have a good team, the players were *trying*, then people would start to believe again and things would get better.

"I was delighted. I'd never heard of a coach letting the press into the locker room right after a game. That was always a time when the coach and the players were alone. So at first, I was pretty careful about what I used."

In Dye's second year, Auburn lost a very tough game to Tennessee. Auburn was behind, and driving, when time ran out with the ball on the three-yard line. Snow went into the locker room and filmed Dye's talk to the team. Later, he was editing the tape when Dye came into the studio to watch. He saw himself saying what he'd said before to his players, many of whom were weeping.

"I wish there was something I could tell you to make you feel better," he was saying, "but I can't. I know it's eating your guts out, but that's life."

"Pat saw me cutting that stuff out," Snow remembers, "and he said, 'Why don't you use that?' "

"I said, 'Are you sure?' "

"He said, 'That's what I told 'em. Put it in.' "

The show, and Dye, have been successful. Two years after he took over a losing team, his team finished third in the final polls, losing only one game. That was in 1983, Auburn's best season in twenty-five years. The Associated Press named Dye Coach of the Year. He had raised the hopes of Auburn fans and was challenging the University of Alabama for football supremacy in the state and, to many, it looked as if he had it within his reach. He never played for Bryant, the way Perkins did. But he worked for him for nine years as an assistant coach and, as a coach, Dye recalls Bryant far more than Perkins does. At times, especially on his television show and during speaking engagements, he seems to *talk* the way Bryant did.

Charley Thornton, who was Bryant's co-host on television for many years, at one point left the state but then returned. One Sunday he was home and the television was on, though he was not watching it. Then he heard a voice that sounded familiar enough to give him chills. He had to listen a long time and look at the picture before he could be sure it was not his old boss, Bryant, but Pat Dye. "I said to my wife that it was eerie listening to Pat. He sounded so much like Coach Bryant that I couldn't pay attention to what he was saying. The way he talked just got to me so much."

If Bryant's passing left a vacant throne in the state, then Dye is trying mightily to inherit it. And to many, it looks as if he might have a chance.

But he will have to win in two weeks.

He tells Snow, at the close of his highlights show, that to beat Alabama, his team will have to play its best game of the year. "We've got to be ready for them, Phil," he says, "because I know Ray's going to have his ready for us."

Then, like Perkins, he leaves for his office, one hour east on the interstate, where he will meet with his assistants, look at films, and try to get ready for the biggest game of the year.

While Perkins and Dye are at work, people around the state are watching their highlights shows and talking about the next game, the big game, the *only* game for many of them.

The Nature of
the Feud

Army/Navy, Texas/Oklahoma,
Ohio State/Michigan, Notre Dame/Southern California,
Harvard/Yale . . . traditional college football rivalries big
enough for sportswriters to call them "classics." These
games seem to capture the essence of college football. During these games, life as it is otherwise lived simply stops
for the faithful. One hundred thousand people old enough
to vote will be totally transported. For three sweet hours,
their whole universe will be one hundred yards long.

Of all these rivalries, Alabama/Auburn is the most resonant, the most intense, the game with the most meaning
for the fans of both schools. Gil Brandt, who scouts college
football players for the Dallas Cowboys and has seen
hundreds of college football games, says that Alabama/
Auburn is easily the greatest of the traditional rivalries.
Keith Jackson, who does ABC's college football telecasts,
agrees. "There's nothing else like it," he says. Ray Perkins
says that it is the most important game in the country. He
has, admittedly, played in this game. But he has also played
in two Super Bowls.

Alabama/Auburn has much in common with the other big rivalries. There have been many years when one team or the other went into the game still in the running for a national championship, and many years when both teams were highly ranked. But that is not always the case. For a rankings showdown, the Ohio State/Michigan game is probably more significant. Or Texas/Oklahoma. Since 1950, there have only been three years in which one of those teams did not finish in the top ten.

Like the other famous rivalries, Alabama/Auburn produces some memorable upsets and, in a year when one of the teams is down and nearly out, the fans can pray for such an upset to redeem the entire season. But for that sort of game, nothing matches Army/Navy. In that game it can be a sort of paradoxical advantage to be the underdog. Favorites almost always win in the Alabama/Auburn game.

There have been some wild, high-scoring games of the sort that leave fans and players limp when the clock ticks down and the thing is over. Games full of long runs, trick plays, and spectacular drives. But only a handful. For this sort of game, the Notre Dame/Southern Cal rivalry is probably best. As Beano Cook of ABC once said, "There has never been a bad Humphrey Bogart movie and there has never been a boring Notre Dame/USC football game." There have been some boring Alabama/Auburn football games.

Finally, among the things this game is not, is it is not the wildest college football game in terms of fan behavior. That distinction would probably belong to Texas/Oklahoma, which is played in Dallas every year. Fans from both schools seem to lose whatever restraint they might otherwise feel. They get drunk and rowdy, get in fights, and get arrested. They also break things. One year, the visiting fans from Oklahoma began throwing desks, lamps, and chairs from their hotel room windows. This is still remembered as "The night it rained furniture in Dallas."

There is very little rowdiness at Alabama/Auburn games. Less, in fact, than at some of the other games on either team's schedule. The game is family. It is played in Bir-

mingham, which is neutral ground and home to many of
the players and fans.

The key to this game is the fact that it is between neigh-
boring clans. And southern clans, at that.

Southerners, in general, believe in football. A writer from
Tennessee once observed that, "Southerners don't think
anybody else can *really* play football. Even when they're
losing to a team from the North or the West, they still
don't believe those people truly understand the game. I
think it goes back to the Civil War. We lost, but we had
the best soldiers. Ohio State and Southern Cal and all the
rest of them have big stadiums and lots of money and
millions and millions of boys playing high school ball. But
we've got the players."

Whether that view is correct or not, it is beyond argument that a lot of Southerners cling to it just as fiercely
as they once held to their belief that one Confederate in-
fantryman was the equal of five—or maybe seven—Yankees and that if it hadn't been for a lack of heavy industry
and a little bad luck at Gettysburg things might have worked
out differently.

In Alabama, this feeling runs stronger than anywhere
in the South. Perhaps because the University of Alabama
was the first southern school to go forth and whip the
Yankees at football, on their own turf. That memorable
day came in 1921. Back then, Confederate veterans still
held reunions—the last one was in 1932—and while the
wound had healed, the scar was still plain. The Alabama
football team went north to play the University of Pennsylvania, a powerhouse of the day. Grantland Rice called
the game "a breather" for Penn. Alabama won, 9–7, under
a coach who was dying of cancer.

The team returned like a conquering army and was welcomed by a delirious crowd at the railroad station in Tuscaloosa. It was as if a score had been settled. A small white
sign that read "BAMA 9, PENN 7" was posted on a drugstore
in downtown Tuscaloosa and remained there for more than
twenty years. It still means almost that much for the Al-

abama fan when the team beats one of the big northern schools.

Alabama was the first southern team to go to the Rose Bowl and those teams, more than any, established the football tradition in the state. A tradition that seems to endure, and to grow even stronger, while so many others vanish in the making of the "New South."

Football is also important because, for so many years, there wasn't much else to depend on if you lived in Alabama. During the Depression, when Alabama's normal state of poverty had reached the acute stage described by James Agee in *Let Us Now Praise Famous Men*, with its haunting Walker Evans photographs of hollow-faced children and their despairing, beaten parents, the University of Alabama was sending football teams from Tuscaloosa to Pasadena to play in the Rose Bowl. Those teams were, perhaps, the single source of pride for people who couldn't be sure they would ever have anything else to be proud of.

Dr. Joab Thomas, the president of the University and a Harvard graduate, once said, "It wasn't until I started getting letters from people that I understood just how important this football team was to them. But when you think about it, it makes sense. This is one place where Alabama is second to no one. Where else does Alabama rank number one?

"So they're proud of the team. It's *their* team, even if they never went to school here and they work for a coal company or a steel mill. It is genuine, this feeling. And if you're in my position, you have to respect it. And I do."

So football itself is important in Alabama. It may be as important in some other parts of the country, but it is absolutely safe to say that it is nowhere *more* important. In the mind of many Alabamians, football is almost a tribal skill and it is of huge importance that *"We* can beat *them* at it." *Them*, of course, being anyone who was not *we*.

And, also, because it was a poor state, football meant opportunity in Alabama. A boy who could play in high school might get a chance to play at the University and

from there . . . well, no telling how far he might go, in
football or out of it. There was one boy from Dothan in
the twenties, who went up to the University to play football, as a halfback, and became a star first at that and then
in the movies. His name was Johnny Mack Brown and he
got a screen test when the Alabama football team went
out to California to play in the Rose Bowl in 1924. From
the University he went to Hollywood, where he starred in
dozens of cowboy films.

And, of course, if football didn't lead to something so
dazzling, it could certainly free a boy from a life of grinding
rural poverty. The state was full of men who had done well
in business or the law or medicine who had first gone to
the University primarily to play football. Bear Bryant himself had been nothing but a dirt poor farm boy from Moro
Bottom, Arkansas, and by the time he died, he was rich,
powerful, and so famous that the President held a dinner
in Washington to honor him. Bryant said he "owed it all
to football." And when he said that, people knew that what
he meant was he owed it all to *Alabama* football.

Sometimes you hear people wondering aloud what it is
about this sport that makes it so appealing in Alabama.
Why not basketball, like in Indiana, where boys grow up
shooting baskets and dribbling instead of blocking and
tackling.

The answer is probably that the military discipline of
the sport and its physical aspect first claimed the affection
of people in Alabama and similar places. The states that
seem to produce the football players are those where hard
work and tough discipline are routine things, where football practice beats working in the mines or the mills, as
in Pennsylvania, or on the farms, in Alabama. And then,
once football takes hold, success breeds success, and success feels good. Alabama is one of only six schools that
have won more than six hundred football games. And no
school has gone to more bowl games.

So boys start early and, by the time they are in high
school, they are playing in front of large crowds, and sometimes the entire town. For the last thirty years, high school

games have been played at night, under the lights of little stadiums all around the state. A Navy pilot, flying on a night cross-country hop out of Pensacola, looked down on the state from 20,000 feet and thought to himself, Hell, you could navigate the whole state of Alabama by the light of football fields.

The towns follow those high school teams with intense pride. The largest structure in town, excepting the Baptist church, will most likely be the high school stadium and, on Friday night, it will be packed with people hoping to see their boys beat the boys who came over by bus, that afternoon, from the next town down the road. Every town has its own quarterback club, which will meet during the week for lunch, just like the Lions and Rotarians. During the lunch, awards will be presented to the players of the week and the coach will stand up and talk about the game that his team just played and, also, the one coming up this Friday night. If it is a good year, he will talk about the team's chances of making the playoffs for the state championship in its division. If he has star players, he will talk about the college coaches who have been around. His remarks will be discussed around town, at the café, the gas station, the barber shop, the mill, and the feed store for the rest of the week. As will the fortunes of boys who grew up here, and whose people are still here, who have gone on to play football at Alabama or Auburn or in the pros. During these discussions, someone will inevitably remember how a boy who is all-pro now and earning more in one year than his daddy made in his whole life, "just had it, you know, even when he was just a little old sophomore and didn't weigh a hundred and fifty with the pads on. But you could see he had it. Even then, little like he was, that boy loved to *hit*. You could see it. Why I remember the year we beat Foley. . . ."

Alabama, then, produces football players. They come out of every little farming and logging town in the state, some of them so small that one recruiter remembers being surprised to find out that there was a boy playing good football in a place that, after ten years of crossing the state, he had never heard of.

"Take you the better part of a day to drive from Mobile in the south part of the state to Decatur in the north," a former assistant coach and recruiter at Alabama says. "A coach at Southern Cal can get in his car, drive an hour in any direction and cover an area where there are ten million people. There aren't a lot of us, so we have to work harder." If a boy is playing good football in high school in a little town in Alabama, then the University of Alabama and Auburn University are going to fight hard to recruit him. Schools like Southern California and Miami can attract players from across the country by promising them the good life. Alabama and Auburn work on a boy's sense of loyalty.

Few of the boys who play well in high school leave the state. Occasionally one will go to Nebraska or Florida or somewhere other than Alabama or Auburn. But this is rare. Most of the players from both schools are from the state. Many played against each other in high school. Or with each other. Many are friends and grew up in the same town, so their parents are friends.

But in a way, a boy would be making a less dramatic and final decision if he chose to leave the state and play for, say, Notre Dame than he does when he chooses either Alabama or Auburn over its rival. That choice is harrowing for a seventeen-year-old living and playing football in the state of Alabama.

In the first place, if a boy is good enough, he will be recruited heavily by both schools and it will be hard for him to say no. It is hard for seventeen-year-olds to say no to their elders in Alabama. Harder still if the seventeen-year-old is a football player and the person he has to say no to is a grown man whose first name is Coach. Imagine a Marine recruit saying no to his D.I.

But, sooner or later, the boy will have to say yes to one school and no to the other. When he does, he will be saying no to some of his friends, his teachers, perhaps his own high school coach, and even to some members of his family. And none of them will consider his decision an unimportant one. He is not choosing between Ford and Chevrolet in this matter, but between the two main branches of the same culture. Within the state, there are Alabama people and there are Auburn people. Commerce, cordiality, and even marriage exist between the two, but the distinction is never truly overcome or obliterated. Something remarkably like clansmanship is at work here, and Alabamians, perhaps because their ancestors were Scots and Celts, embrace these loyalties fiercely.

Two years ago, a pass receiver who was heavily recruited by both schools was told by his parents that the decision was his to make. He thought and thought and finally decided to go to Alabama. His parents accepted the decision and it was in the papers. Then, a few days later, his mother spoke to him. She said she was sorry, but she just didn't think she could stand it if he went to Alabama. She'd gone to Auburn and everyone she knew had gone to Auburn, and she just didn't think she could stand it. So the boy changed his mind and went to Auburn.

Because Auburn is the agricultural and engineering school, the easy generalization is that its people are farmers, small shopkeepers, surveyors, and the like. The yeomen of the culture. The University of Alabama, the capstone university, on the other hand, can be abstractly thought of as the place where the sons and daughters of establishment people go and become educated, more or less, before becoming bankers, lawyers, men of affairs, and ladies of society.

The cultural model might go something like this:

In a small town just below the black belt of Alabama (so named for the color of its alluvial soil, not its citizens), there is a bank. The president of the bank will be, of course, a graduate of the University. His father, who founded the bank, would also have gone to Tuscaloosa. The banker's sons and daughters will go there when they finish high school. One of the bank's best customers will be a man

who owns several hundred acres of good farmland just
outside of town. He will raise Angus cattle, grow beans
and wheat and even a little cotton. He will have a small
pecan orchard and a couple of catfish ponds on his place
and, in the touch-and-go world of agriculture, he will be
"doing all right for himself." He will be an Auburn man.
So will his sons, one of whom plays high school ball and
might be good enough to get a scholarship. All things being
equal, Auburn will get him.

The boy's father, as mentioned, will borrow the money
he needs for planting from the Alabama man who runs the
bank. He will buy his seed and fertilizer from an Auburn
man who runs the fuel and feed store. When his live-
stock needs shots he will go to an Auburn vet. An Alabama accountant will help him through the ordeal of his
taxes.

The county sheriff will be an Auburn man. Doctors, if
there are any, and lawyers will likely have gone to Alabama. The foresters and county agricultural agents will
almost certainly be Auburn graduates. If our farmer needs
insurance, he can go to a graduate, and perhaps a former
football player, from either school.

As the size of the town increases, so will its distinctions.
A newspaper editor now working in Washington, D.C., remembers when he started on the *Dothan Eagle*, the daily
paper in the largest town—and Johnny Mack Brown's
town—in what is called the "wiregrass" portion of the
state. "It was remarkably clear-cut. Everyone in editorial
was an Alabama graduate and everyone in the print shop
was Auburn. You could hardly make a big status thing out
of it since they were union and made a lot more money
than any of us. They certainly didn't feel inferior to us and
I know I never felt superior to them. It's just that they
were all Auburn and we were all Alabama and in the days
just before the game, we were riding each other all the
time. Their way of life, you know, against ours. It's that
way all over the state."

Government—political power—in the state is oddly divided. Sheriffs are most often Auburn men. Judges are likely to be products of Alabama. For the last quarter of a century, the governor was usually George Wallace, who went to Alabama. But the populist side of George Wallace has attracted more Auburn people than Alabama graduates to the capitol in Montgomery. The people who run the programs are primarily from Auburn.

There was only one four-year period since 1962 when neither Wallace nor his wife were governing the state. In 1978, a man named Fob James was elected over a man named Bill Baxley. James was not only an Auburn graduate, he had also been a star halfback at the school in the early fifties. Auburn beat Alabama on the football field the last two years James played.

During the campaign, Baxley, who graduated from Alabama, circulated ads claiming that Bear Bryant was against having an Auburn man in the governor's mansion. It would be bad, Bryant said, for Alabama football. In many states, a secondhand endorsement from a football coach would not have amounted to much. But in Alabama, the ads set off a minor storm of controversy. Bryant was accused by supporters of James and by some who were merely good government types of "meddling in politics." Which, of course, he was. There would have been no controversy except for Bryant's stature. He was easily the single most towering figure in the state. There had been rumors, in earlier years, that he was considering a political career himself, perhaps with a campaign for the U.S. Senate. Nobody doubted he would have won against anyone, including Wallace, who also talked about the Senate.

So the concern wasn't merely that Bryant was "meddling." It was that he might actually swing the election. But in the end, Bryant's influence turned out to be insufficient for Bill Baxley's needs and Fob James was elected governor. If that added prestige to the Auburn football program or gave it an advantage in the recruiting struggles, the difference was marginal. Alabama and Bryant beat Auburn in each of the four years James was in office.

The sociology of the Auburn/Alabama rivalry is not clear-cut. But people who know the state have no trouble understanding it. When the city of New York had three baseball teams, each team came to stand for the characteristics and values of its fans. The Yankees were Manhattan. The Giants were the Bronx. The Dodgers were Brooklyn. All sorts of sociological baggage was carried into a Yankees/Dodgers world series. The same thing is true of an Alabama/Auburn football game . . . except if your team loses, there is no East River to separate you from your enemies. You live among them, do business with them, see them every day.

"If your team wins the game," a student of Alabama football said, "then for the rest of the year, everything is just a little bit easier. And if your team loses, then everything you do will be just a little bit harder until they play again."

Speaking to a group of football boosters, Bear Bryant once said, "Sure I'd like to beat Notre Dame, don't get me wrong. But nothing matters more than beating that cow college on the other side of the state."

His remarks were reported in the papers and, a few days later, a fired-up Auburn team upset the heavily favored Alabama team that was undefeated and looking at a national championship.

The "cow college" crack was probably a slip. Bryant was too shrewd to give a team he was about to play that kind of emotional incentive. His usual method was to praise the other team to the skies and to talk about how outweighed, undertalented, and badly hurt his own players were. But when he called Auburn a "cow college," Bryant was only saying what every true Alabama fan thinks.

This feeling finds expression in Auburn jokes, a kind of down-home version of Polish jokes. When Fob James was governor, the joke was that you could be sure he'd gone to Auburn because he spelled *Bob* with an *F*.

The basic Auburn joke is the one that goes like this:

Q: What is a seven-course dinner at Auburn?
A: Stewed possum and a six-pack.
Or,
Q: Do you know why they play on natural grass at Auburn?
A: Because the cheerleaders need a place to graze.

And so forth. Some of the jokes are very elaborate and a few are even funny. There is more than a little meanness in some of the jokes and the people who tell them. The smugness of Alabama people is especially galling at Auburn because it seems so . . . well, *unearned.* Alabama may have the law school and the medical school, Auburn people will tell you, but the majority of students in any entering class will have done their undergraduate work at Auburn. Furthermore, Auburn students test higher nationally, place more people in prestigious graduate schools, and win more academic honors. Auburn is the only school, except for the service academies, that put both a pilot and co-pilot on the same space shuttle. In 1985, Auburn received contracts that made it the primary research institution for President Reagan's "Star Wars" missile defense system. *"Auburn,* not MIT," say people who go there and are fiercely proud of the school and resent its reputation as a mere "aggie school."

Alabama, in Auburn's view, is nothing but a party school for rich kids who don't know how to do anything but spend Mama and Daddy's money. "They talk about Auburn people wearing overalls and driving tractors," Coach Pat Dye said, somewhat bitterly, at a press conference last year, "when the truth is we also write books and go to the moon."

Auburn people, in other words, believe they are as good as anybody. The jokes, which they hear, make them want that much more to prove it.

The first Alabama/Auburn football game was played in 1893. It was played in Birmingham, as it still is, and Auburn sent 226 fans while Alabama was represented by 320.

The proportions are more or less the same today. The newspaper account read, "Never before was there such enthusiasm over an athletic contest in the state," words that would be appropriate in just about any year. Auburn won the game 32–22.

The two teams managed to play irregularly for the next fifteen years, which was something of an accomplishment in those times. College football was in its infancy, but even so public an advocate of the strenuous life as Theodore Roosevelt joined its critics after seeing a photograph of a badly mauled Pennsylvania player named Maxwell. Roosevelt's criticisms led to rules changes and the formation of what has become the NCAA.

The early Alabama/Auburn games were hard fought and earned their share of controversy. Before the 1894 game, Auburn claimed that Alabama was using players who had already suited up for North Carolina that season. The two accused players were suspended, but another two, which Auburn claimed were paid hands and not even remotely legitimate students, played, presumably contributing to Alabama's 18–0 victory.

In those days, it was common for schools to bring players in from distant places—the Pennsylvania coal fields were especially popular—pay them for a few games and send them on their way. There were itinerant college football players who went from school to school, doing what they were paid to do and then moving on. It was not unusual for university teams to field players who could barely speak English but were fluent in some Slavic language and good with their fists. Cheating in college football is nothing new.

The game in those days could be brutal and, occasionally, the violence would get out of hand altogether as the fans joined in, ganging up on a player they thought was carrying things too far and beating him with canes, umbrellas, fists, and even chairs and benches. Riots followed some close, especially intense, football games. Disputed calls by officials were frequently the catalysts for these brawls. Umpires, as they were called then, were routinely suspected of taking bribes.

At one point, the University of Alabama virtually gave up football because the game had become so thoroughly tainted. But, after two years, the trustees were forced by student pressure to reconsider their decision.

It is not surprising, then, that when Alabama and Auburn stopped playing football against each other after a 6–6 tie in 1907—and did not start again for forty years—all sorts of stories would be told, and believed, around the state to account for the situation. The last game played between the two schools, according to these stories, had been too brutal for anyone to even *consider* playing it again. Why, there had been fights all over the field and a full-scale riot off the field. People had been seriously injured. Maybe even killed. The two schools just couldn't play each other again. It was too dangerous.

The more the stories were told, the higher the pitch of agitation to resume the series. Organizations like the American Legion would pass regular resolutions urging the two schools to get together and schedule a football game again. People drafted petitions, wrote letters to the newspapers, made speeches, and did all the usual things to see if they couldn't get some action, but for forty years, the two teams did not play each other and the stories grew more fantastic, even lurid.

The truth is almost embarrassingly humdrum and pedestrian. It turns out the schools quit playing each other in 1908 because they got into an argument about money. (That, too, was a factor in college football way back then.) Auburn thought $3.50 *per diem* was about right for the players it would be bringing to Birmingham that year. The players would be staying in a hotel and eating at restaurants, after all, and Alabama was the host team. Alabama thought that was about fifty cents too high. Also, they didn't see the need for Auburn to bring the twenty-two players they said they needed. Twenty, Alabama thought, ought to be plenty. And then there was the matter of how

to choose an official. The schools couldn't agree on one
from the South and, to break the impasse, Auburn sug-
gested turning the question over to a committee. Alabama
refused at first, then agreed after compromises were reached
in the disputes about *per diem* and squad size. By the time
the last necessary compromise had been made, however,
it was too late to schedule a game that year.

For the next forty years, officials of the two schools nursed
a grudge and the wild stories came to seem more and more
plausible, though the Auburn coach of the last game, played
in 1907, remembers it as a clean match, with the fans
generally behaving themselves. He could recall no significant mayhem on or off the field.

Finally, after the Second World War, when colleges were
once again fielding football teams and fans were starting
to feel the fever, political pressure was brought to bear.
Representatives in the Alabama legislature threatened to
attach riders to the bills providing funding for the two
schools that required them, by law, to play a football game
against each other. University presidents, then and now,
know a threat to their autonomy when they see one. There
was no need, they quickly said, for this kind of hasty, *political* action. Gentlemen ought to be able to take care of
a small matter like this without duress. After a secret
weekend meeting, held on a farm about halfway between
Tuscaloosa and Auburn, a game was scheduled for 1948.
Once the details were worked out, the presidents of the
two schools' student bodies met in a Birmingham park
where they buried a symbolic hatchet.

That afternoon, Alabama beat Auburn 55–0.

Auburn nursed that humiliation like an insult to family
honor and, the next year, upset Alabama in one of the most
memorable games of the series, 14–13.

Many in the state remember something about every game
that has been played since then. And some games, of course,
stand out. There was the time Auburn won 10–8 with a
backup quarterback, holding off Joe Namath himself. The
time Ken Stabler ran nearly fifty yards in the mud to win

7–3 against an Auburn team that even Bryant admitted should have won.

And then everyone remembers the 1972 game. Remembers what happened, anyway. It was the wildest game in the series. The game that proved most dramatically how much chance, fate, fortune and all the other "intangibles" they talk about really mean in football.

It was the year after Pat Sullivan won the Heisman and graduated, along with his favorite receiver, Terry Beasley. So Auburn was supposed to be rebuilding.

But the team won. By the time of the Alabama game, Auburn was 9–1, better than anyone had guessed they would be when the season began.

Alabama, however, was 10–0. Ranked number two in the nation and chasing the number one ranking, Alabama was heavily favored to beat Auburn and for three quarters it looked like things would go exactly that way. Alabama scored an early touchdown, missed the extra point, then scored another touchdown and kicked a field goal. Auburn was unable to move and kicked a long field goal with ten minutes left in the game. Auburn fans booed the decision, but Shug Jordan said later he didn't see where he had a choice. He needed some points and Alabama had been stopping them all day. With the fourth quarter winding down, it was 16–3, Alabama.

Then . . . Auburn's Bill Newton blocked an Alabama punt. The ball bounced into the hands of his teammate, David Langner, who ran twenty-five yards for an Auburn touchdown to bring the score to 16–10. Auburn, excited now, kicked off to an Alabama team that could not move and was forced once again to punt. On the sidelines, Bryant considered using his number two punter, who was quicker. Everyone felt like if they could just get the punt off, the defense would hold Auburn. But the number two punter had just ripped the nail off the big toe of his punting foot. He limped so badly when he ran onto the field that Bryant called him back and sent the regular punter in.

Up in the broadcast booth, John Forney said to Doug

Layton that it looked like the Alabama punter was setting up awfully shallow. The ball was snapped. Again Newton broke through and blocked the punt, and again the ball bounced into the arms of David Langner, who ran it, this time twenty yards, in for the score.   .

In the huddle before the extra point, a wild Auburn player screamed to the kicker, "If you miss it, I'll kill you. I swear it. I'll kill you."

The kick was good: 17–16 Auburn on two blocked punts, run back for touchdowns, in the fourth quarter. Bryant took his defense, which had held Auburn to eighty yards rushing, aside and said, "Gentlemen, I apologize. If we had put the ball on the five-yard line and given their offense all afternoon to score, they couldn't have done it. We lost because of bad coaching and I apologize."

All over the state signs and buttons and bumper stickers appeared bearing the words "Punt Bama Punt." Almost fifteen years later you will still see one of those stickers, now and then, on an old, rusted pickup. *Punt Bama Punt.* It is a three-note musical chorus for any true Auburn fan.

Coach Jordan called that team "my Amazings." He said that he had always declined to pick out any one team as his favorite before, but now he was going to. The Amazings were his choice. His favorite team ever. There were no stars on the team. Running back Terry Henley probably came the closest. But they were a real team. After beating Alabama, they went on to the Gator Bowl where they were supposed to lose to Colorado by eleven points. But they won there too. Final record, 11–1. Final ranking, number five.

Alabama, demoralized, went on to lose to Texas in the Cotton Bowl. Bryant spitefully benched the regular punter. Alabama finished number seven in the ranking. Behind Auburn. *Those two blocked punts. . . .*

At some point Auburn coach Shug Jordan began calling the game the "Iron Bowl," which was an accurate reflection of the spirit of the game as well as the town where it was played. In those days, Birmingham was a tough, dirty, hard-nosed steel town that rested in a valley surrounded by mountains full of red ore. The mountains are still there, though much of the iron is gone, and the mills are mostly closed. The largest employer in Birmingham today is a university medical center.

But the game is still called the Iron Bowl. And the one that will be played two weeks after Alabama's win over Southern Mississippi and Auburn's over Georgia will be the fiftieth in the series. Up to now the series stands at 29–19–1, Alabama's way. But those are all old games. This year's game is the thing.

On the day of that game, there will be no weddings scheduled in the state of Alabama. All year long, the sports desks of the state's newspapers answer calls from people who want to know what day the game is scheduled for. They're getting ready to get married and they want to make sure people will come to the service.

Regular golf foursomes will not play on that Saturday. The only one they will miss all year, even if Christmas should fall on Saturday.

People will plan their vacations around the game.

For the two weeks leading up to the game Alabama fans will taunt their friends from Auburn. At a hospital in a small city, the doctors from Alabama will repeatedly page the one staff doctor from Auburn to tell him the latest Auburn joke, bringing him out of surgery, on one occasion, to tell him the one about how many Auburn graduates it takes to eat a possum.

Auburn fans will retaliate, reminding Alabama fans that Auburn is a three-point favorite and is ranked number eight in the polls while Alabama is nowhere in the top twenty. They will taunt Alabama people about the game against LSU when Ray Perkins decided to kick an extra point to tie the score after a late touchdown instead of running or passing for a victory.

"Did you know Ray Perkins is an only child?" they'll say.

No.

"That's right. His parents decided not to try for two."

In bars there will be long, friendly arguments. And some that are short and not so friendly. Somewhere violence will erupt, get totally out of hand and someone will be killed.

Though both coaches will close practice to visitors and the press, the sports pages will be dominated by news of the game. Player interviews. Coach interviews. Accounts of memorable games in the series.

It will be just about impossible for anyone living in the state to get through an entire day without hearing about the game. By kickoff, the suspense will be all but unbearable and wonderfully so.

Big Bowls, Big Stadiums

Late Sunday morning, after his television show and his recruiting breakfast, Ray Perkins sits in his office chewing tobacco and answering phone calls from reporters and the representatives of various bowl games. Alabama would be playing in a bowl game, but at this point just about the only certainty is that it would *not* be the Rose Bowl. For the last forty years, that game has been reserved for the champions of the Midwest's Big Ten conference and the West Coast's Pac Eight. No southern teams. Now and then you can find an Alabamian who still thinks this is because the Rose Bowl people are chicken.

Alabama has a long shot chance at the Sugar Bowl, which automatically invites the team that finishes first in the Southeastern Conference. But for Alabama to win the conference, Tennessee must first lose to either Kentucky or Vanderbilt and LSU must lose to Notre Dame or Tulane. There is a chance, but it is remote. Nor will Alabama be going to the Cotton Bowl or the Orange Bowl. These are the New Year's Day games, the "major bowls." From 1961 to 1981, Alabama appeared in one of these games seven-

teen times. Travel agents around the state began putting
together bowl packages and counting on the business. But
this year's team is not ranked in the top twenty. It has lost
to Tennessee and Penn State, both by two points, and tied
LSU. The seven games that it won were not enough to win
an invitation to one of those prime, New Year's Day games,
especially since most experts expect the team will lose to
Auburn. Wherever they go, fewer of their fans will follow
them. Bad for the travel agents. But Auburn fans might
pick up the slack. . . .

Perkins answers the phone. "No, we haven't made any
commitment yet."

He listens and, while he is listening, spits into a paper
cup.

"Well, we're talking to the Liberty and the Aloha and
the Cherry. I'm meeting with the seniors right after lunch.
We'll discuss it and then they'll decide. It'll be up to them."

He hangs up the phone. His large, walnut desk is clean.
If he turned just slightly to his left, he could look out a
picture window at the football practice field. There is a
painting of Bryant hanging on one of the dark paneled
walls. A sofa and chairs are arranged for conference in one
corner of the office. The carpeting is thick, subdued crimson and gray. It is an office that would satisfy just about
any CEO. Rich, sturdy, and masculine. The only thing that
gives it away as a coach's office is the film projector and
screen set up in one corner of the room for Perkins's use.
No coach is ever very far from a film projector.

The office takes up the prime corner of a two-year-old
building that is the headquarters of Alabama football. From
the outside, it is all cool red brick and dark tinted glass.
Inside, it is soft carpeting, floor-to-ceiling hardwood doors,
and thick walls that absorb noise and keep things so quiet
that when you enter the building you do not think sports—
shouting, naked athletes, ranting coaches, the clanging of
weights, and the running of showers—but business, computers, organization, and money.

The building cost almost six million dollars. It houses,
in addition to Perkins's office, the locker rooms, weight

rooms, and training rooms used by the football players. They are clean and modern. No other athletes may use the facilities. If a swimmer or basketball player wants to lift weights, he goes to the Coliseum next door. This is the house that football built.

There are also radio and television studios, with all the necessary outlets and plugs, for player interviews. And large meeting rooms for the offensive players and defensive players. Smaller meeting rooms for the coaches. Offices for all the assistant coaches. Each office is equipped with a movie screen that can be raised or lowered from the desk. Coach doesn't even have to get out of his chair and cross the room if he wants to watch some film. "Can you believe *that*," one of the assistants says. "At most schools, the assistants don't even have offices."

Perkins is convinced that it is "the finest football facility in the country. I sure don't know of one that's any better."

When he took over as head coach, and then as athletic director, things weren't in such good shape. A member of Perkins's staff says, "Things had really deteriorated under Coach Bryant—and you've got to understand that I'm not knocking the man. He was the greatest ever, but he wasn't interested in improving facilities. He hated spending money."

While Auburn was modernizing and adding on to its stadium until it was the biggest and finest in the state, the stadium in Tuscaloosa deteriorated. It hadn't been painted in years and seated some 20,000 fewer people than the one in Auburn. It was, by comparison, a relic. Perkins had it painted and spruced up. But that was cosmetic; his main concern was the new football facility.

"When you bring a player to campus to recruit him," Perkins says, "the *last* thing he asks to see is the stadium. He's only going to spend a few hours there every year. He wants to see the athletic dormitory, the weight room, the locker room. He's going to be living in those places. Not in the stadium."

He takes another call. "Hello."

He spits again as he listens.

"I understand Auburn has already made a deal with the Citrus because the Cotton has made a deal for the runner-up in the Big Ten."

He listens again.

"Uh huh. Well somebody was trying to make a three-way deal with us, LSU, and Tennessee for the Liberty, the Gator, and the Sugar."

All of this must be done today, even though most teams have at least one game left to play this season and some have as many as three. But according to the rule book, this is the day when bowl deals are made. Formal invitations are extended, and accepted in one week. A team that holds off accepting a bid from a minor bowl game in hopes of finishing as conference champion, and thus being automatically invited to a major bowl, is taking a chance. If Alabama refuses all minor bowl bids and Tennessee wins the conference, Alabama might not go anywhere.

But the rush to accept bowl invitations leads to some strange pairings. It is even possible that this year a team with a losing record might play in a bowl. Southern Cal will be playing in the Aloha Bowl. They have one game left and, if they lose it, their record will be 5–6. Of course, this is no stranger than the fact that Southern Cal will be playing its last game, against Oregon, in Tokyo.

Bowl games pay as much as a million dollars and as little as one-third of that. They are played in cities as various as New Orleans, Miami, Detroit, and El Paso. Bowl games are considered, in part, a reward for a good season, a chance for players and fans to go somewhere and have fun. You can have more fun in Hawaii than Detroit. But you make less money. These are all matters that Perkins and his seniors must consider.

While Perkins talks about the bowl situation, his visitor admires the office. Perkins has had several visiting high school players in his office this morning to talk to them and try to persuade them to come to Alabama. The office is a selling tool. In the competition with Auburn for recruits, virtually everything is. The school that wins the competition plays in a New Year's Day bowl.

For years, that school was routinely Alabama. As long as Bear Bryant was alive he got the best players in the state. "He creamed the crop," one of his assistants said. Auburn did the best it could and went out of state, to Georgia and parts of Florida, for some of its best players. Late in the sixties, Auburn did beat Alabama in the state and won the big game two straight years. In the seventies, Bryant and Alabama won the recruiting battle and the football games—nine between 1973 and 1981. But in Bear Bryant's last two years, Pat Dye had thoroughly outrecruited him.

Now, Dye and Auburn were challenging Alabama and Ray Perkins for football supremacy in the state.

Last year's game had been a critical moment in this struggle. Alabama in Perkins's second year had won only four games and lost six going into the Auburn game. Auburn had won twice as many and was on the verge of winning the conference championship and going to the Sugar Bowl for the second straight year. For the first time in twenty-five years, Alabama would not be playing in *any* bowl game, a fact that would not be lost on high school players around the state. Three straight victories over Alabama and a second straight holiday trip to New Orleans would help the Auburn recruiting pitch tremendously.

So Auburn was favored to win the game. And the expected win might just turn things, once and for all, their way.

But Perkins's team played tough and, midway through the fourth quarter, actually led the game 17–15. Then Auburn intercepted an Alabama pass and returned it to the seventeen-yard line. A few plays later, Auburn had the ball on the Alabama 1, fourth down, with less than four minutes remaining in the game.

The conventional decision would have been for Auburn to send on its kicker and try for a field goal. That would have put them ahead by one point. Everyone in Legion Field expected it. But the kicker stayed on the sideline. Auburn was going for the touchdown. It was an unorthodox decision, but one that fit the personality of Pat Dye.

"Running the ball down Alabama's throat," someone who knows Dye said later, "would have given him more satisfaction than all the field goals in the world."

So he did not send the kicking team in and, when Auburn came up over the ball, everyone in the stadium and everyone watching the game on television expected Bo Jackson, Auburn's best runner, to carry it, probably up the middle, over the top. Though Auburn had been outplayed, Jackson had gained more than one hundred yards and, in the fashion of the great running backs, seemed to be gaining strength as the game went on.

But Jackson did not get the ball. Worse, he did not hear the signals and, as the play unfolded, ran to the left while all the other Auburn players—including Brent Fullwood, the ball carrier Jackson should have been blocking for—went right. Fullwood was naked and the Alabama safety came up and rode him out of bounds for a loss.

"I waxed the dude," Rory Thomas, the safety, said after the game.

Alabama got the ball, couldn't move, and had to punt. Auburn had one last chance, missed a long field goal and lost the game and the chance to go to the Sugar Bowl. Instead of New Year's in New Orleans, Auburn went to Memphis for the Liberty Bowl, a cold, second-echelon game.

Jackson going the wrong way without the ball . . . Fullwood thrown for a loss. It became *the play* and, almost immediately, an Auburn joke. Fourth and dumb. How do you get from Auburn to Memphis?

Go to the one-yard line and turn left.

And so forth.

Auburn fans turned on Dye. Turned on Jackson. Perkins, who had clearly outcoached Dye even before the play, was given a temporary reprieve by Alabama fans and, according to the experts, recruited an excellent class of freshmen. The win had certainly helped in that. It may have saved his job and held off the Auburn challenge for another year. Now he and Dye were even in head-to-head competition. The total score of the two games was 38–37, Alabama. Auburn in the Dye era was 2–2 against Alabama.

The 1985 game would give Auburn a chance to regain the momentum it had lost when Bo went the wrong way on fourth and one. Or, it could turn things decisively Alabama's way again and leave Auburn in a second best situation that would be familiar but that much more bitter for how tantalizingly close they had come . . . one yard. Fourth and one, and Bo goes the wrong way.

"It was a long season," Dye said almost nine months after the play. "And that game, that *play*, made it an even longer off-season."

The word that everyone who has ever played for him or with him uses to describe Pat Dye is "tough." Nobody ever starts out by saying he is "determined," or "smart," or "intense." Always "tough." A former Alabama player who remembers Dye from when he was an assistant there says, "Pat was tough. Real tough. He didn't just want to win football games; he wanted to beat the other guy physically so he knew he'd been whipped. That's the thing Coach Bryant liked about him. Pat was a good coach, and a smart coach, but Coach Bryant liked him because he was tough."

Dye was an All-American guard, playing for the University of Georgia in 1960. According to a man who coached him there, "Pat played harder, and was more competitive than anyone on the squad. I remember one year when we were playing Georgia Tech, and that was in the Bobby Dodd era, when they had great teams and were our strongest rivals. We were ahead seven, nothing, but Tech scored a touchdown late in the game. They lined up to kick the extra point and we *had* to block it to win the game. So we put Pat, who usually played inside, at guard, outside at end and told him to go for the block. He did, and he gave it everything he had, and by God . . . he blocked that kick. We won the game seven, six. Pat was that way. Real tough. Never been anyone more competitive."

But he was also an academic All-American, which was unusual at Georgia, where coach Wally Butts positively hated the classroom side of college and considered it sissy stuff and a waste of a ballplayer's time. Dye, who had grown up on a poor Georgia farm, had to stand up to his own coach to study and make his grades.

Though he is the head coach of Auburn, Dye learned his coaching at Alabama from Bear Bryant. He was an assistant to Bryant for nine years and left only because it was beginning to look as though Bryant might never retire. Certainly not in time for Pat Dye to get a chance at his job. If he was ever going to be a head coach, then he would have to leave Alabama and Bryant.

He went to East Carolina in 1974 and put that school on the football map. He was an "us against everybody" sort of coach, which Bryant had been, especially in his early days. In the same season, Dye beat both of the state's big schools—the University of North Carolina and North Carolina State. Before each of those games, he looked at his players in the locker room and asked how many of them had been offered a scholarship by the school they were about to play. One or two hands would show and Dye would then say, "Well, that's what they think about *you*. Now you go out there and show them what you think about *them*."

Dye left East Carolina in 1979 and went to the University of Wyoming. The school had its first winning season in years. A year later, the Auburn job came open. Dye wanted it, but first he called his old boss in Tuscaloosa.

Bryant told Dye he thought it would be bad for him to take the Auburn job.

It was a great opportunity, Dye said. One that might not ever come his way again.

You couldn't be too sure about that, Bryant said cagily. Maybe Dye should stick it out in Wyoming for a few more seasons. Bryant was then in his sixties and no one knew for sure, probably not even Bryant himself, how much longer he would be head football coach at Alabama. Dye was already one of his most successful protégés and was sometimes mentioned as Bryant's successor. But Bryant wasn't making any promises over the phone that day.

"Coach," Dye said, "you don't know what it's like out

here. You can drive two days, recruiting the state, and never see a tree." Dye, who was born in Georgia, was homesick.

"Pat," Bryant said, "if you come back here, to Auburn, I'm going to whip you."

"That may be, Coach," Dye said. "But I'll tell you this. Whoever comes after you, I'm going to beat him like a stepson."

So Dye came back to the South, took the Auburn job, and the first time his new team played Alabama, he lost. And that Alabama victory was Bear Bryant's 315th as a college football coach, which broke one of those records that was supposed to stand forever.

The next year Dye's Auburn team beat Bryant's Alabama team 23–22. After the game, Dye said he was pleased for his team, but that he took no special pleasure in beating his old boss. No pleasure at all.

Bryant retired less than two weeks after that game. And in another month, he was dead. A huge vacuum had been created in Alabama and, in many ways, Pat Dye looked like the man to fill it. He mumbled when he talked, just like Bryant. He was a tough physical coach who liked to win with defense, just like Bryant. He recruited the "mamas and the papas," just like Bryant. He was a country boy who liked hunting and fishing, just like Bryant. When his team lost, he always said it was the fault of "poor coaching," just like Bryant. He won football games, just like Bryant. And though he'd been an academic All-American (as well as a football All-American), he liked to play dumb . . . just like Bryant.

"He's getting more like the old man every day," says Alf Van Hoose, who is the sports editor of the *Birmingham News* and has been covering Alabama football for as long as anyone can remember.

"Bryant used to say that he was just a dumb country boy who didn't really know anything. Shoot, the people who believed that, *they* were the dumb ones. It's the same with Pat. He might be a country boy, but he sure isn't dumb."

Dye is spending his day doing what Ray Perkins is doing. But Dye is getting a little bit better class of caller. At least one of them is a major bowl. The Cotton, which is played in Dallas, could not get the Big Ten team it wanted in order to boost its television ratings—many more sets in Michigan than in Alabama—and is now looking for some other way to attract viewers. Auburn has a likely Heisman trophy winner, the same Bo Jackson who went the wrong way the year before. If he does win the Heisman, then he will attract some viewers and add some Nielsen points. It helps that Auburn is number seven in the rankings. If they beat Alabama they will go up. If they lose . . . well, best follow the example of the Aloha Bowl committee and not think about that.

Still, even though the Cotton Bowl is calling, the season has been a disappointment for Dye. . . .

Before the season began, Auburn was a solid contender for the national championship, an almost certain bet to finish first in the Southeastern Conference. Bo Jackson was picked by the experts to win the Heisman trophy. He was routinely compared to Herschel Walker, the great running back who set so many records at Georgia and won the Heisman in 1982.

Auburn fans dreamed extravagant dreams of a conference championship, a Sugar Bowl bid, a national championship, a Heisman trophy winner, and a victory over Alabama. In the past, they had been blessed with all those things separately. But this year . . . this year, by God, they were going to have it all. And they could thank Pat Dye for leading them to glory.

Dye is a popular man in Alabama. He is as familiar as Perkins is mysterious. Dye likes to hunt and fish. One Auburn fan who owns a large farm in the black belt invites Dye down for some quail hunting every year after the season is over. "He's just good folks," this man says of Dye. "He likes all the good country things and he won't put on any airs with you. He's just Pat Dye. Nobody is going to talk about running him for governor and you won't see him keeping company with movie stars. He's folks."

Dye's agreeable nature has worked to his advantage. The Auburn fans like him, of course, but so does the press. At a meeting of Southeastern Conference coaches and the press, in Birmingham before the season began, he mingled more than any other coach and he might have been the only coach there who actually enjoyed himself. He has the gift of asking the question you want him to ask and he is either genuinely interested in what other people have to say or he has enormous political skills.

He stood near the center of the room with a drink in his hand. He wore a sport jacket and a golf shirt and he looked tanned and relaxed, like a man just back from a few days at the beach. He spoke to reporters he recognized and when one stopped to talk, Dye asked the man what he'd been up to.

"Well, I just sold a book, Pat."

"You did, really? Hell, that's great. I didn't even know you were writing one. Tell me about it."

The man describes his novel, which is set in Montgomery where he had worked for a newspaper during the days of the bus boycott.

Dye listens, attentively. Then he says, "I'll bet it took you a long time to write that."

"Yeah, Pat. Nineteen years."

"I'll bet you wanted to quit an awful lot of times, didn't you."

"Oh man."

"But you didn't. And that's great. I don't believe I could stay with something that long. I admire you for doing that. It took real guts."

"Well thank you, Pat."

"Let me read that book sometime, will you?"

"Sure. I'll send a copy to your office."

"Do that, will you. I mean it."

After Dye has moved away, the man who has written the book says, "You know what. That sumbitch right there *will* read my book." Just then, he'd play linebacker for Pat Dye, even though he is close to fifty. "He's probably the only coach in this room who has read any book in the last five years. He's a damned good man. I'd like to see him go all the way."

And for the first two weeks of the 1985 season, it looked like he just might.

Auburn blew two weak teams off the field and Jackson ran for more than two hundred yards in each game. Auburn was ranked number one in the nation and it was just late September, still early in the season. Bo—as he was called by everyone in the state—looked to have a lock on the Heisman, which would be awarded on December 7, one week after the Alabama game. Auburn fans could hardly wait.

But first, the team had to go up to Knoxville to play Tennessee. The game was to be a showcase, Bo's first performance of the year on national television.

Auburn lost, embarrassingly, 38–20. Bo gained a mere eighty yards and took himself out of the game in the third quarter, saying that he had hurt his knee and, anyway, he wasn't helping the team. It was a performance that raised questions about Jackson's character, questions that would follow him all the way to December 7, Heisman day. Ballplayers, especially Heisman-winning ballplayers, do not walk off the field because they are having a bad day. The conventions, which are rigid in these matters, require that nothing less than an injury will excuse you and that injury must be severe enough that you are carried off the field.

There was one interesting and widely remarked sidelight to the story of the game. People who follow football in the deep South wondered all week long how Jackson would do against the Tennessee defense because the coach of that unit was Ken Donahue, a strange, eccentric man even within the fraternity of football coaches, almost all of whom are fanatics at the very least.

Ken Donahue had been an assistant to Bear Bryant at Alabama for nineteen years. He was routinely considered a defensive genius. It followed, almost logically, that he was also a strange and somewhat difficult man. He liked to wear Sherlock Holmes–type hats and he needed glasses— eyestrain, no doubt from watching too much film—but he also had the face of a boxer who had been moderately successful as a counterpuncher. His nose was so flat that his glasses were never properly supported and they were always leaning a few degrees, either way, from the true vertical. Donahue looked like what he was, a deep scholar of a violent game.

He knew his specialty as well as anyone alive, and he believed in himself . . . totally. He would argue with anyone, which was all right on Bryant's staff, because everyone *knew* who had the final word there. Donahue stayed on at Alabama after Bryant retired and Perkins took over. Bryant is supposed to have worried aloud that "Ken and Ray won't be able to 'gee' and 'haw' together."

They couldn't. Perkins offered Donahue an office job in the athletic department and a nice raise after their second year together. Donahue refused it, quit, and went to Tennessee.

While he was at Alabama, Donahue had recruited high school prospects, just like any assistant coach. One of the players he tried to interest in Alabama was Bo Jackson.

There are many stories in the state about why Jackson chose to go to Auburn instead of Alabama. According to one, Donahue told Jackson that he would not start at Alabama until his junior year and if he went to Auburn, he could "count on losing to Alabama for the next four years."

Jackson went to Auburn. In the three years he ran against Donahue's Alabama defenses, Jackson averaged 168 yards a game. Donahue became known as the man who let Bo Jackson get away. Probably no one felt worse about it than Donahue himself.

The Auburn/Tennessee game, then, was the last chance Donahue had to stop Jackson. After the game he said, "I was glad to see Bo standing on the sideline in the third quarter, and I will be even gladder to see him graduate."

Auburn dropped from the number one position in the polls. But there was still a chance of getting back there by the end of the season. The conference championship was still a real possibility along with the automatic Sugar Bowl bid that came with it. Bo might still win the Heisman and, certainly, Auburn could still beat Alabama in the season's biggest game. But Tennessee was a bitter disappointment. Pat Dye admitted that, three games into the season, he was still not settled on a quarterback. Some Auburn fans wondered what kind of coach left that question unsettled going into October and the meat of a tough schedule.

But both the team and Bo came back in strong, convincing fashion. There were easy wins over Mississippi and Mississippi State. And tough, impressive wins over Georgia Tech and Florida State. Auburn climbed back up in the rankings to number seven and then it was time to play Florida, which was undefeated and ranked number two in the nation.

Many experts considered Florida a good bet to finish the year as national champions, making them one of three teams to accomplish the feat while on NCAA probation. The last had been Oklahoma in 1974. Ironically, this unhappy distinction also belonged to Auburn in 1957.

The game was played at Auburn. From all over the state, fans came to watch the game, to wear the orange and blue, and to line the street that led from the athletic dormitory to the stadium cheering wildly as the team walked down to dress for the game.

It was a close game and a tough game. Very tough. Auburn went ahead 10–7, but Jackson was having trouble making yardage. Once again, he took himself out of the game. This time with a thigh bruise. In the fourth quarter, Florida drove the field, scored, and won the game 14–10.

"There weren't no place out there," Pat Dye said, "for women and children." Except for the score, it was his kind of game. Fundamental and tough.

But if Dye took it well, Auburn fans and Heisman voters did not. At this point in the season all hope of a national championship was gone. The conference championship was a remote, nearly forlorn dream. Likewise the Sugar Bowl. Bo was running away from the Heisman. That left the Alabama game.

Around the state, people told Bo Jackson jokes. You heard

about the new kind of Auburn ice cream? It's called the Bosicle. Two licks and it's gone.

There were others, even less funny, and some that were simply cruel and racist. Auburn's mascot was no longer the war eagle, ran one. They didn't need it since they already had a black chicken.

There was also widespread criticism of the Auburn offense and its coordinator, Jack Crowe, a man who had never played college football and who, in the opinion of many, did not make good play selections under pressure. The feeling was that Auburn counted too much on the run and hard-nosed defense. That might have been good enough for the sixties and seventies, but in the eighties you needed to pass, like Ray Perkins was doing over at Alabama. Perkins had coached in the pros and he knew the offensive game. Auburn was stuck with a head coach whose first love was defense and whose second was the running game. Plus an offensive coordinator who was easily rattled. The good feeling and high hopes of the pre-season were gone.

Auburn and Jackson played indifferently against East Carolina. They won but satisfied no one. The season seemed on the verge of disaster in spite of the fact that one more win would make the last four years—the Bo Jackson years—the most successful in Auburn football history.

But expectations had been so high . . .

The two teams Auburn still had to play were Georgia and Alabama. It seemed entirely likely that they could lose both games. Even Coach Dye admitted that would make for a "less than average season." He said it with unconcealed concern in his voice and his face.

Georgia, with the best defense in the Southeastern Conference and the third best in the nation, would be tough. Furthermore, the game would be played in Sanford Stadium, in Georgia. The stadium was beautiful, but the Georgia fans could be the loudest, most hostile in the South, with the possible exception of the fanatics who lived and died for LSU. Georgia fans did love their Bulldogs. "How bout them dawgs," is accepted as a formal greeting in Georgia. Growling, as one says it, is optional.

The game would be on national television so, once again, Jackson would have an opportunity to impress the Heisman voters. If Bo were to win the trophy, he needed to have a very big day. But he was coming off an injury. The thigh bruise that had taken him out against Florida had limited him to seventy-three yards against East Carolina the next week. Auburn trainers said that he had only 60 percent flexibility in his injured leg. He did not practice, according to reports, at all in the week before the Georgia game. Jackson himself said he expected to be about 90 to 95 percent healthy for the game.

Pat Dye knew all this, but he was confident, just the same. The night before the game, he said he liked his game plan, which was simple and perfect for his own temperament. "We plan to close it up and go at them," he said. "Everyone else has been trying to spread them out, but we're going straight at them."

It worked. Auburn won, convincingly. And Bo ran for more than one-hundred-and-twenty yards on nineteen carries with two touchdowns.

One of his touchdowns started sixty-seven yards from the goal line. He took the ball, went outside, broke a tackle, hesitated for just a second, then cut back across the field on a diagonal and was in the clear. He ran and, as he accelerated, the pursuing players fell visibly behind. This run succeeded on equal parts of speed and agility.

The shorter touchdown came from inside the ten-yard line and Jackson ran straight ahead, through a good hole. But there were two defenders between him and the goal. He hit one of them straight ahead and went over him without losing either his momentum or his balance. Hit him so hard you could feel the impact high up in the stands and, if you liked football, it felt good. Contact like that was the whole point of football for men like Pat Dye; it was the reason you played the game.

The second man got his arms on Jackson, but there was way too much power for one man to contain. Jackson broke easily into the end zone. He had been making runs like that for three years, almost four now, but these two were made against the third best defense in the country. They looked routine and almost easy for him.

"This is as great a win as I've been involved with in some time," Pat Dye said happily.

"I'm just going to let the Heisman take care of itself," Jackson said.

"After the way he played today, hurt, against that defense, I'd say yeah, he deserves it," Dye said.

Vince Dooley, the Georgia coach, agreed.

In the night, outside Stanford Stadium, Auburn fans shouted "War Eagle," and "Bring on Bama." They painted "We Beat the Dooley Out of Them Dawgs" on their car windows in soap. It had been a disappointing season in many ways, but now things seemed better again. Bo could still win the Heisman and, better, the team that beat Georgia so soundly ought to beat Alabama when they played in two weeks. And that, more than anything, would make it a sweet, sweet season.

A major bowl game would be almost enough sugar to chase away any last bitterness.

The rumor that night is that Alabama has accepted a bid to the Aloha Bowl contingent upon their *not* being invited to the Sugar Bowl and that Auburn, meanwhile, has agreed to play in the Cotton Bowl against either Texas or Texas A&M, a team that Alabama has already beaten. The rumor, it turns out, is true. Auburn fans are delighted and Alabama fans are disappointed. Hawaii is too far away and too expensive for many of them to make the trip—especially to see their boys play against a team that will have to fight to be six and five.

It has now been five years since Alabama last appeared in a major bowl. Auburn, on the other hand, has appeared in a major bowl two of the last three years. Auburn has never lost a bowl game with Dye as coach.

If there is competition between the two schools in football facilities, stadiums, coaches' shows, bands, and everything else you can think of, then there is competition over bowl invitations.

And this year, Auburn wins that one too. Even before they have played the Alabama game.

"But they still have to win that one, and I'll tell you something. We're going to whip those country bastards and then we're going to the Sugar Bowl," an Alabama assistant coach tells a private meeting of boosters at a meeting in Birmingham that night. "And then on New Year's Day, the Cotton Bowl is going to be a game between two leftover turkeys."

The World of
Boosters

Every Monday during the
football season, the Birmingham Quarterback Club meets
for lunch. There are several hundred members, all male,
all well connected, all—needless to say—avid football fans.
Both for Alabama and Auburn, but probably more Alabama. The Quarterback Club has, in almost forty years of
existence, raised five million dollars for charity. A building
at the downtown medical center was funded largely by
the Quarterback Club and is named accordingly.

The club's good works are undeniable, but the men who
join do so for reasons that have more to do with football
and the kind of fraternity it provides in the South than
with charity. In Manhattan, there are regular lunch clubs
where members share insights into the most important
aspect of life there—getting ahead, making it, achieving.
The Quarterback Club, likewise, is organized around the
most important aspect of life in Alabama—football.

Members serve themselves from a buffet and take seats
at tables. There are printed forms listing the major college
football games coming up that weekend. Members mark

the teams that they expect to win and try to predict the
scores of two or three games. These will be used as tie-
breakers. This is the "poor picker" contest. Each week
there is a winner—this week's expert picker wins a por-
table radio—and each week there is a loser. He wins a
toilet seat.

As the members eat, there is an auction. Donated items
include one crimson telephone and one orange one, Alabama and Auburn colors, respectively. Also a belt buckle
and a gaudy, tropical looking necklace of shells. There is
much hooting and laughter when the emcee attempts to
sell this last item for sixty-five dollars. When the bidding
starts on the orange telephone, one man says he'll pay two
hundred dollars for it if the guest speaker, who is Ray
Perkins, will use it to call Bo Jackson at Auburn and tell
him which way to go. Perkins's face breaks into a rare,
toothy smile and he says he figures that by this time, Bo
probably knows which way to go. The telephones fetch
more than two hundred dollars each.

When the auction and the meal are over, it is time for
the guest speaker, Perkins, to be introduced. The man who
makes the introduction is a former teammate named Jerry
Duncan. Probably no living former Alabama player is held
in more affection than Duncan.

He was a teammate of Perkins's. The teams they played
for won national championships in 1964 and 1965. They
were undefeated and untied in 1966 but were ranked third
behind Notre Dame and Michigan State, which had played
each other to a 10–10 tie that still galls Alabama fans.

Duncan was a running back in high school. He didn't
have the ability to start in the backfield in Alabama, so
Bryant moved him around trying to find a position for
him. Duncan was short on talent but long on the other
things that Bryant looked for. Bryant described these players like this: "First there are those who are winners and
know they are winners. Then, there are those who are
losers and know they are losers. Then, there are those who
are not winners but don't know it. They're the ones for me.
They never quit trying. They're the soul of our team."

Duncan finally played as an offensive tackle. One who caught passes off a trick play called "tackle eligible." Just before the snap of the ball, the man outside of Duncan would step back from the line of scrimmage, making him a flanker back. The man who had lined up on the other side as flanker back would step up to the line of scrimmage, making him an end. Duncan would also be an end for that play and, hence, an eligible receiver. He caught a lot of passes and actually ran one for a touchdown. "I thought they were going to call me for delay of game," he says. "Man, I was *slow*."

The play was eventually outlawed.

Duncan played aggressive, feisty football. This was in a time when Bryant liked players who were small and quick. On these teams of "little bitty boys," Duncan sometimes gave away fifty pounds to the man he was trying to block.

"He liked to cut his man down, go at him around his feet," one of his teammates remembers. "Once he got the guy, he'd start riding him, trying to get him rattled. Jerry's like that. Real competitive. If he's beating you, he just wants to beat you worse. We were playing LSU one year and they had some huge guy across from Duncan and this fellow was pretty good. But for a while, Duncan had his number. He'd cut him down and while he was lying there, Jerry would say to him, 'How'd you like that, you big Cajun sumbitch.'

"That guy looked across at Duncan after one play and said, 'All right, you, sometime during this game I'm going to get your little ass.' Well, a few plays later, Duncan comes back into the huddle and his helmet is knocked all sideways so that he's just about looking through the earhole of the thing, and there's a little trickle of blood coming from out of his mouth. He says, 'Boys, why don't we run a few at the other side of the line. The way that sumbitch handled me, they'll never expect it.' "

Duncan wasn't professional material. The most he ever weighed was one-hundred-and-eighty-five. So he stayed on at Alabama working on his master's degree and as an assistant coach for Bryant. He might have stayed in coaching

except that he developed severe, incurable rheumatoid ar-
thritis in his feet. There was so much pain that he could
not stand on the sidelines for the length of a game. The
condition worsened until the joints between his toes and
feet had to be removed. He was in surgery repeatedly for
several years and had to walk with the help of a cane. He
wasn't yet thirty years old.

Bryant helped him get a job in securities. He is now
Dean Witter's Birmingham man in tax-exempts. His medical problems have lessened and, though he still limps, he
can play tennis and pickup basketball at the YMCA.

"You've never seen anyone more competitive than Duncan in those games," a friend of his says. "He goes down
there and plays with guys who are half his age and bigger
than he is by a full head and twenty pounds. And he gets
right in there with them. Runs them to death. The next
morning you'll see him and he can hardly walk. In the late
afternoon, he'll be all right. Ready to go again."

Duncan is healthy enough to have made it back to the
sidelines. He is part of the radio broadcast team that does
the Alabama game over the radio, interviewing players
and coaches during the game. Even on the air, he refers
to the Alabama team as "we."

The previous Saturday, in Bryant-Denny Stadium, Duncan was on the sidelines as usual when a Southern Mississippi player ran out of bounds. He came right for Duncan,
hit him low, and took his legs from under him. Duncan
went down in a heap but jumped right up, almost as if he
were looking for someone else to block. Everyone in the
stadium saw it.

"Y'all probably saw me last Saturday," Duncan says,
as he begins his introduction of Perkins. "I was over there
on the sideline, doing the broadcast, when this big old
Mississippi boy came over and liked to kill me. What you
probably didn't see was how I got up, slapped him on the
butt, and said, 'Nice play.' He looked down at me and said,
'Well you old *fool.*' "

The audience appreciates this. Pure Duncan.

"It is a great honor for me to introduce our guest speaker

today. We came to the University of Alabama together, in 1962, as two of nineteen fullbacks recruited that year. Because he was a great athlete with tremendous speed, our speaker was moved to one of the skilled positions, wide receiver.

"Because of *my* athletic ability and speed, I was also moved . . . to tackle."

More laughter.

"Our guest went on to the pros where he played in two Super Bowls and then into coaching where he became head coach of the New York Giants. I became a graduate assistant coach at Alabama until my feet gave out on me."

Duncan has the entire room laughing by the time he finally introduces Ray Perkins. When Perkins stands and comes to the podium, every man in the room also stands and applauds. This is the head football coach of the University of Alabama. Some of the men in this room are enemies of Perkins and want him fired. But the rule is, you respect the position.

Perkins is smiling. He looks relaxed and thanks Duncan for "that fine introduction." He reminds the men in the audience that "Duncan caught passes, too. And he's probably the man most responsible for getting the tackle eligible play made illegal."

Applause.

"We still have something at the University of Alabama that goes back to our time there. It's called the 'Jerry Duncan, I Like to Practice Award.' I can't recall ever seeing him smiling or laughing in practice, but I guess he must have. I've been trying to figure out who to give the award to. I haven't found anyone yet. I hope I don't. If you like to practice, there's something wrong with you. Just look at Duncan."

Bear Bryant remarked once that you had to order Jerry Duncan not to practice, even when he was hurt, and once, when he was told he couldn't practice, Duncan started crying.

Perkins goes on to say some nice things about the Quarterback Club and its good work with crippled children.

Duncan had mentioned in his introduction that Perkins was signing over his honorarium to one of the club's projects. When all of the required things have been mentioned, and the laughter has died, Perkins does what he came here to do, which is talk football for these men.

"I'd like to say, first, that I'm proud of this team. I'm especially proud of them after a big win on Saturday. I feel a lot better standing up here this year than I did a year ago. I don't know where we were last year, at this time, but I know we weren't 7–2–1.

"It's been a great source of pride for me, this year, to watch us come together as a football team. You start out with a bunch of guys and you have to go through some things together before you can be called a 'team.' But we're getting there. We're starting to play with the kind of 'oneness' that we had back when you and I played, Dunc."

He goes on and talks about the improvement of some individual players and finishes by saying, "Now, before I take questions, I suppose I ought to say something about our next opponent." He smiles, slyly, when he says this.

"I think this is the best team, in terms of personnel, in Auburn's history. They've got the big man, as everyone knows, but they also have a great defense and a great kicking game. In order to beat them, we are going to have to play the best game we've played all year."

Nothing is new in this, but it mirrors what everyone in this room believes and what the papers have been saying. With more than ten days to go, the tension is already gathering like the crowd at a street fight.

Perkins takes questions, all of them respectful.

One man asks about the play calling.

"The plays come from the press box and field. The bad plays come from the box and the good plays come from the field."

Perkins is on the field.

Another man asks how Vince Sutton is coming along. It is an interesting question because Vince Sutton had been a prospect of the very first order, a strong-armed quarterback and a *Parade Magazine* high school All-American who was recruited by everyone. Perkins persuaded him to come to Alabama. He played some the year before, as a freshman, when Alabama had its first losing season in twenty-seven years. This year, he has played in only two series late in a game that Alabama won in a runaway. A few meaningless plays. He has not been injured. He is plainly not in favor with Perkins, whose answer is vague.

"Sutton is working in the number two or three place, behind Shula. Dave Smith is going good too. If we need a change, I'll make it."

Everyone in the room would like to know what Sutton has done to get himself so far out of Perkins's favor, but they won't find out here, from him. Later in the week, an assistant says to some Alabama supporters that Sutton doesn't have the mental toughness to play for Perkins, who caught passes in his own career from Joe Namath, Ken Stabler, Steve Sloan, Johnny Unitas, and Earl Morrall and, therefore, has a preference for thinking quarterbacks. Sutton thinks he can win on talent alone and Perkins is not impressed by mere talent.

Somebody asks Perkins about the prospects for next year's season.

"I'm not thinking about next year. Not this week."

Well, another voice comes in, what about recruiting? You are thinking about *that*, aren't you?

Perkins smiles. He spent most of the weekend, except for the game, talking with recruits. He allowed himself ten minutes at a reception for the returning members of the '65 team, his old teammates, before leaving to talk with prospects at Paul Bryant Hall, the athletic dormitory. He stayed two hours and during that time he spoke briefly to each of the prospects. There was a cookout in progress. Steaks on the grill in the small green area behind the dormitory. Many of the prospects were there with their parents and, while they stood in line, Perkins would shake the hands of the fathers and talk seriously about the team and its prospects, then he would hug the mothers and say something flattering. He could have been a candidate working a reception except that he lacked the outright vulgar enthusiasm for his work.

He did not have much time alone with any of the prospects and didn't seem to be looking for that. But he did take one big, fair-faced kid from Enterprise aside, look him in the eye, and say, "I'm going to need you here. I want you to come to Alabama."

"Well, Coach," the boy said hesitantly, "I'd love to come to Alabama but I've got to have a scholarship."

"I'm *offering* you a scholarship. Right now."

"Well . . . ah, well, yeah *great*."

Perkins shook the boy's hand. "You can do a lot for us."

"I'll do my best, Coach."

"I know you will."

When Perkins had moved away to talk to another boy and his parents, the boy from Enterprise quickly found his parents and said something into his father's ear. The man took his son's hand, pumped it, and then threw his arm around the boy's shoulder. The two of them stood like that for a minute or two, not saying anything, simply enjoying the shared satisfaction of a dream come true.

Perkins got that one, that night, and a couple of others. So recruiting has been very much on his mind and at this point, he is confident.

"We're doing all right," he says.

There are a few more questions of no particular consequence. Perkins handles them easily. When he finishes, everyone stands and leaves to go back to the offices where they sell real estate, practice law, write advertising, and the like. On the way out, several of the men remark on how relaxed Perkins seems.

"You remember how he was the first year, when he came here to talk?"

"Hard as a stone."

"Never smiled. Like it would have broken his face."

"He's learning."

"Just like everything else, he's going to *make* himself good at this."

"Well, he has come a long way. This is the first time I've seen him speak when he didn't make a single enemy."

Perkins lingers briefly, then drives back to Tuscaloosa for afternoon practice. That night, he will watch film in his office until almost midnight. He will be back at the office before six the next morning.

While Ray Perkins is studying film in his office, the Birmingham Touchdown Club holds its weekly meeting where the guest is Pat Dye. The Touchdown Club has no charitable goals or functions. "The only thing we raise," says one of the members, "is a lot of hell." Tonight, there will be some of that. But the members will also be interested in hearing what Dye has to say about Auburn's chances against Alabama and about his team's season in general, which has been baffling and disappointing to many loyal Auburn supporters. At 8–2, Auburn has a better record than Alabama. But Auburn fans were expecting much, much more.

The Touchdown Club meets in a room on the ground floor of the downtown Hilton. There is a cash bar. Members and guests avail themselves since it is six o'clock in the evening, cocktail hour in a party town.

Most of the talk is, unsurprisingly, about football. It is hearty talk. Animated by the fact that both Alabama and Auburn have had good seasons and good games this past weekend. Also by the fact that both coaches need the game so much and seem—on the surface of it, anyway—to be such different kinds of men. By the fact, too, that everyone thinks the game will be close. The last three have been decided, after all, by a total of eight points. And, finally, by liquor and normal Alabama high spirits.

It is a good, loud, rousing happy hour.

"Tell me something, do you believe there is any way, after Saturday, that the Yankee press can give the Heisman to anybody *but* Bo?"

"I don't know, there's that quarterback, the one from Iowa."

"Sheeeit. Did you *watch* that game? Did you see that

sumbitch run? And he was running against Georgia, now. The junkyard dogs themselves. He wasn't running against the Sweetbriar Sissies."

"I know."

"I've watched a lot of 'em, back to Billy Cannon, and I believe Bo is the best."

"Better'n Herschel?"

"I never saw Herschel get any tougher yards than them that Bo got on Saturday."

"Maybe so, but he still hurt himself, coming out like that against Tennessee and Florida, when his team was losing."

"And he helped himself, Saturday, against Georgia. *And* he's going to help himself even more, Saturday a week, against Aladamnbama."

"You sure about that?"

"Think about the worst day he's ever had against the Tide, my friend, the very worst. One hundred and fourteen yards. You'll be lucky if he don't double it."

"**W**hen it gets down to the short strokes, coaching is going to make the difference."

"You figure the Tide has the coaching, do you?"

"Believe it shows."

"Well take a look, when you have a chance, at the film of last Saturday's game. On the field goal your boy missed. Count the players on the field."

"Only ten, huh?"

"Nope. *Nine*. That's what great coaching will do for you."

"**Y**ou know, I believe there are two things that this team lacks . . . just two things keeping it from being undefeated and national champions."

"An offense and a defense?"

"Got all the defense in the world. Pat Dye could make the Junior League play tough defense."

"What is it then?"

"We need a quarterback and an offensive coordinator. Until we get 'em, we'll just keep on hitting on seven cyl-

inders, winning eight or nine games a season, losing two
or three . . . it's just a damned shame."

"I can remember a time when winning eight or nine a
season didn't sound so bad to you Auburn people."

"Maybe so. But now we've seen the promised land. . . ."

The doors to the dining room open and the men line up
at the bar for a last drink to carry in with them. The tables
fill and then the room falls briefly silent for an invocation.
After the "Amen" the noise level picks up and remains
fairly high while the winner of the club's poor picker contest is announced. His prize is a "cravat," the emcee says.
"We decided to call it a cravat because if the winner was
an Alabama man, he wouldn't settle for another tie." Alabama fans are still distressed about the LSU game, two
weeks ago, which ended 14–14.

The loser of this contest also wins a toilet seat.

After a few announcements, the emcee calls on Pat Sullivan to introduce Dye.

Sullivan is probably the best known of all former Auburn players. He is the school's only Heisman winner so
far. He won the award in 1971, beating out Ed Marinaro
of Cornell who is now better known for the cop he played
on "Hill Street Blues." In Sullivan's three varsity years,
Auburn beat Alabama twice, won a total of 26 games, and
went to 3 bowls. The years when he was quarterback, running the option and throwing passes to his favorite receiver, Terry Beasley, were easily the best for Auburn
football until Pat Dye arrived in 1981.

Sullivan comes from Birmingham, where his father was
an employee of the power company. He went to a Catholic
high school and was a star player there and very highly
recruited. Alabama sent one or two coaches over from Tuscaloosa to have dinner with him every single week for two
years. But he chose Auburn.

He played briefly in the pros but wasn't the big, tough,
strong-armed quarterback that game needs. So he came
back to Birmingham, where he has been involved in several businesses and currently owns a large tire dealership.

He is an announcer, and a good one, on the radio broad-
casts of the Auburn games. He makes a brief, formal, and
proper introduction of Pat Dye, noting that he is the only
coach ever to beat Georgia's Vince Dooley "three years in
a row."

The men in the room stand and applaud as Dye steps
up to the microphone.

He has a friendly face, with a trace of something a little
wry in it. He looks like a man who wouldn't mind a good
time, like a couple of beers and some stories. Maybe a little
hunting trip in the morning. It is one of those good country
faces that seem to say, "Look here now, you *can* take life
too goddamned serious."

"Well," he says, "thanks for that good introduction, Pat.
And thank all of you for that nice welcome. It's good to be
here." Dye brushes his sport jacket back, like a detective
showing his pistol, and hooks a thumb into his belt.

"It's a good feeling," he begins, "when you're sitting
here with a drink, or two drinks, or a whole bellyful of
drinks. When you're like that, you feel like you can't make
a mistake. So let me tell you about how it feels to make a
mistake. Because I *know*."

Appreciative laughter fills the room.

"Lord, do I know." Dye shakes his head and smiles. It
would be fairer, actually, to call it a grin. When he is
having fun, he grins.

"Take last year's Alabama game. Some of you may remember it. I'd been coaching the wishbone for eleven years
before we get to Birmingham and Bo goes the wrong way.
All of a sudden I'm a dumb sumbitch who don't know how
to coach the wishbone.

"So we went back this year and we put in the I-formation.
Now, if he goes the wrong way, at least it won't look like
it."

More laughter and Dye's grin widens.

"Well," he says, turning serious for a moment, "it's been
another tough year. We lost some close games. Some big
games. They say that in the big games, and the close games,
coaching is what makes the difference. So I guess you'd

have to say I haven't done a very good job of coaching this year."

Somebody at one of the tables whispers, "Damned if he don't sound more like Bryant every year."

"Last week, before Georgia, I was reading all about it. About how Bo ain't got no guts and I can't win big games."

The grin is stretched to the limit now.

"Well, I mean to tell you, last week was a *big* game. And Bo Jackson left his guts all over the field."

As Dye beams, the room is filled with applause and a few wild yells.

"Yes, sir. I told my players, before we traveled over to Athens, that we'd won some games, but that we were supposed to beat most of those teams. That we were going to be judged by how we did against Tennessee, Florida, Georgia, and Alabama.

"And they were ready for us, over there in Athens. They had signs all over the stadium saying all kinds of ugly things. I didn't even want my babies *reading* that stuff."

More laughter.

"All week long Georgia is talking in the newspapers about what they did to Florida and what they're going to do to us. I didn't even tell my team what I normally do— 'If you're scared, don't go.' 'Cause I was afraid I might get there and not have enough to play."

Dye beams and the audience roars. One of the staples of country boy storytelling is an elaborate description of just how scared you were before the fight. Especially if you eventually *won* the fight.

"But seriously," Dye says, "it was a big, big win. And I'm proud for my boys. They needed a win like this one and the way they played, they deserved it."

Sincere applause follows and lasts for several seconds. When it quiets, Dye goes off on another topic.

"It's been an exciting year in the SEC," he says, "and I think the best coaching job in the conference was done in Knoxville by Ken Donahue. Even though Tennessee and his defense beat us, it does my heart good to see that coaching can mean that much to a team. Everybody at Knoxville has done a good job. They lose Robinson, who is an All-American quality quarterback, and replace him with a little old boy who ain't got no talent at all, and they keep right on winning. I think that's good coaching.

"They done a good job at Tuscaloosa too. Ray has done a great job there this year. A lot of people are saying that now, but a lot of them are the same people who last year was out there yelling and raising sand and saying 'You dumb son of a bitch.' "

Laughter and applause follow these remarks. Dye has gone out of his way before to speak well of his rival. It was one of Bryant's trademarks.

From here, Dye wanders off, without any logical transition, to the game against Florida State.

"You know, bad as the crowd was in Athens, they're just about that bad down in Tallahassee." He proceeds to tell a long, rambling story, full of laugh lines, about the time he argued with the officials about a call and was penalized twice for unsportsmanlike conduct.

"So that's when I look to my offensive coordinator. You need to have someone you've got confidence in, for a situation like that. 'Jack,' I said. 'You got a play for first and fifty-five.' "

Wild laughter.

"But I'll tell you, Florida State is tough and they can run the reverse better than anyone in football . . . especially when they clip. I saw the clip. And I went over to the official and I said, 'He clipped.' The official said, 'I know he did.' 'Well then, throw your flag,' I said. 'It wasn't my call,' he says, and boys, that's when I knew we were in for a long day."

More laughter.

" 'Course any time you think coaching is easy, just remember how it was for me, last week, before Georgia. I had Bo with his leg hurt so bad that he couldn't practice and Brent (the other tailback) comes down with the hemorrhoids. Bo's riding the bicycle and Brent's sitting in the whirlpool and I'm trying to get ready for Georgia without no tailback.

"Middle of the week I come home, growling and raising sand, and my wife, Sue, says to me, 'Well what's wrong with *you*?' I couldn't even tell her. The next day, I told Brent that we were going to put a rubber band around that thing just like they did to George Brett in the World Series. He says, 'No, Coach, don't do that. I'll be ready in one more day.'

"So the next day I come in, still ain't got no tailback that has practiced all week and I got to play Georgia in two more days. I see Brent still in the whirlpool and I picked up a big bucket of ice and dumped it in there with him. He starts screaming and I said, 'Come on out of there, son, I need you more than that thing does.' "

After much wild, appreciative laughter, Dye again thanks the men in the room and says once more that he is proud of his team and he knows they'll have to play a good football game, a complete football game, a week from Saturday. " 'Cause I know Ray is going to have them ready. I'm just going to have to do my best to have mine ready, too.

"Goodnight. Thank you."

On his way out of the dining room, leaving the Hilton to catch a plane to some small town in northwest Florida where he wants to talk to some recruits, Dye shakes hands and accepts the greetings, compliments, and affectionate back slaps of the men who were at the dinner. Then he runs into Terry Henley. Before anyone can stop it, the two are having words and, from the looks of it, are not far from blows.

Terry Henley is a former Auburn halfback who last played in 1972. He was All-Conference on a team that upset Alabama in perhaps the most memorable game of the series. He is a Birmingham insurance man now and something of a public figure around the city and the state. He is a strong critic of Dye and his offensive coordinator, Jack Crowe. Like many Auburn fans, Henley believes that Auburn plays too conservatively on offense, that if they opened things up they might be undefeated and number one. Henley has made his feelings known in radio interviews and, lately, in a letter that was made public. In the letter, he said Auburn would keep losing big games until it got rid of "that dog Jack Crowe."

Now, when Dye sees Henley he tells him what he thinks of the letter.

"You're just hurting Auburn and hurting yourself when you say things like that, Henley."

"What did I say?"

"Calling somebody a dog."

"I didn't call him a dog, I called him a 'Collie Dog.' " Henley smiles.

"You know what I mean. I just wonder if you know what you're doing." As he speaks, a faint tinge of red rises in Dye's face. One of his assistant coaches pulls at his arm.

"Come on, Coach. We got to go."

"I wonder if you know who you're hurting, Henley."

"You think," Henley says, "that if I cut my veins I don't bleed Auburn?"

"If you cared that much, you wouldn't be doing what you're doing."

"Come *on*, Coach."

Dye's jaw is thrust toward Henley and his feet are spread. He is ten years older than Henley, who is whippet thin but still looks strong.

As the crowd around them grows and presses in and someone whispers, "Pat will kill him," Henley turns away smiling and the assistant coach finally persuades Dye that he really ought to go catch that airplane.

The episode is over. But if Auburn loses to Alabama, there will be more like Henley. And they will be raising their sights. Jack Crowe will not be their only target.

Watching Film

Tuesday afternoon, and the teams are back at work. From now until game day, practices will be held in secret. Padded green material is hung on the wire fences that surround the practice fields at both schools. What the players and the coaches are working on behind those green walls—new formations and trick plays—will provide the raw material for thousands of hours of speculation between now and kickoff.

Both schools use huge speakers to broadcast the recorded sounds of an excited crowd at a football game so the players will be accustomed to hearing it. Coaches yell and blow whistles. Bodies collide with bodies and astroturf. (Legion Field is a turf field and practices are run under the closest thing coaches can get to game-day conditions.) A foreigner walking by one of those padded green walls and hearing the sounds might imagine that whatever is going on behind them is just too brutal for some eyes.

Stick 'em, stick 'em, stick 'em. Block that kick, block that kick. Go . . . go . . . go. Thud. Crack. Attttaway. Huddle up, huddle up. Run goddammit, run. Take it to him, take it to

him. Uh. Huh. Arrrrrrgh. Good play. Good play. Thataway.
Let's go. Get 'em again. Arrrright defense. Dig . . . dig . . . dig.
Go for that ball. Reverse . . . reverse. Draw . . . draw.
Bingo . . . bingo. Take it to 'em, take it to 'em. I told you to
run, goddamnit. Now get over there. Drive . . . drive . . . drive.

It does seem brutal when you can only hear it. But for
some people, like Pat Dye, who turned forty-six three weeks
before the game, the practice field is the place to be on an
autumn afternoon. To celebrate, he got down in a three-
point stance and blocked a man less than half his age with
a forty-pound weight advantage. Doing it just like he did
it for Georgia when he was an All-American guard and
linebacker in the late fifties.

"Felt good," he says later. "Real good. I may look old,
but I don't feel old."

Dye is the kind of coach who gets down with the players,
grabs their face masks and shakes them to get their attention. Puts his face right up next to theirs and yells at them
to make sure they get the message.

Ray Perkins's birthday is the same day as Dye's. He
doesn't do anything special to celebrate. "Maybe I looked
at an extra roll of film," he says. "I don't remember."

Perkins, who was tough as a player, is more cerebral
than Dye as a coach. He studies the game, mercilessly
watching film. Running it over and over, looking for the
edge.

"Coach Perkins," says one of his assistants, "finds something before every game. We all watch film, but he sees
more than the rest of us. That's why he's the boss."

The week before the season began, against Georgia, Perkins sat in his office after a hot afternoon practice talking
with a visitor. He was waiting for one of the team managers
to bring him his supper in a paper sack. It was one of the
many nights during the season when he ate at the office.

The visitor asks him what he would be doing, staying
there so late. It was still August, school hadn't even started.

"I've got to look at the film," Perkins says. It is plain he
thinks the question barely deserves an answer.

The visitor asks, a little nervously, if Perkins will show him how a coach looks at film.

With nothing else to do before his breaded pork chops on a styrofoam take-out plate arrive, Perkins shrugs, saying all right and moves over to the corner of his office where the little projector is set up and the film is already threaded.

He turns the machine on. Grainy images flicker against the screen. The film is color but there is no sound. It reminds the visitor of old newsreels. Coaches spend a large part of their time looking at film like this. It cannot be anything but tedious.

"Okay," Perkins says. "This is Georgia playing Mississippi last year. Georgia on defense. In this situation, the linebackers will blitz and the corners will be one on one. Watch the receiver down in the lower part of the screen."

The visitor watches. The ball does not come to the receiver, who goes deep.

Perkins stops the projector. "See it?"

"What?"

Perkins does not answer the question. He runs the film backwards and stops it when he is ready to show the same play again. "Watch the receiver."

The visitor watches the receiver.

"Now," Perkins says. He stops the projector.

"What am I looking for?"

"What's the receiver doing?"

"Running?"

"Yeah. But which way is he looking?"

"Right there, he's looking back upfield."

"Right. Now watch it again. Look for what the corner back does when the receiver does that."

The visitor watches. It happens—whatever it is—so fast, the first time, that Perkins has to run the film back and show the play again.

"See the way the corner makes a little move when he sees the receiver looking back?"

"Oh, yes."

"Well, he's cheating. Just a little. He thinks the receiver is looking for the ball and he's going to cut in front of him for the interception."

"Right."

"So what happens if that's just a little fake and the receiver takes off, right now, for the post."

"Well, he ought to be open. Especially if he's fast."

"That's right. And Al Bell is very fast." Bell is a junior college transfer from California, recruited by Perkins. His first game for Alabama will be against Georgia, a few days off. It will be played at night and broadcast by ABC.

Perkins runs through the play again and again, until the visitor can see what he sees and imagine what he must be imagining, which is Al Bell looking back and, when the defender takes the fake, turning upfield, in the clear, and waiting for the pass to come to him.

On Labor Day night, the visitor watches the game on television and it happens exactly that way.

"That guy is Georgia's best defender against the pass," an Alabama assistant says later. "In our first coaches' meeting we started talking about how we were going to have to work on the other defenders and Coach said, 'No. We're going right at him.' He found out how you do it."

But . . . there isn't much chance that the Auburn game will be decided on something like that. This is the last game of the season and there are not many secrets or surprises then. Both teams know each other.

Past games have turned on single plays, but they are not the kind that coaches come up with in the film room. They come from the players. The two blocked punts. A run of nearly fifty yards, by Ken Stabler, on a muddy field to win it 7–3 for Alabama. A short pass from backup quarterback Mailon Kent to All-American Tucker Fredrickson, to win it 10–8 for Auburn. A missed extra point by Ed Salem, giving Auburn a 14–13 game. A missed signal by Bo Jackson.

Planning and study, then, probably will not win the game. Still, the coaches plan and study and worry over injuries. Bo Jackson's leg, which looked all right against Georgia but isn't entirely healed.

Alabama's punter broke his leg stopping a return against Mississippi Southern. It isn't his kicking leg and Perkins thinks he'll play.

"Nobody wants to miss this game," he says. "If he can possibly kick, he'll be in there."

Bear

On Wednesday morning, ground is broken in Tuscaloosa for the Paul W. Bryant Complex. The centerpiece of the complex will be the Bryant museum. The complex will also include a hotel and convention center.

The ceremony is quiet but well attended and widely reported. It could not be otherwise. The name Bryant still resonates in Alabama with a force that is almost beyond language. When you say Louisiana, people think *Huey Long*, mention Mississippi and what they hear is *William Faulkner*. From now on, when you say Alabama, they will see that big man in the hound's tooth hat. He was a giant and, three years after his death, his proportions have already grown. He has become even larger in myth than he was in life.

They used to say that the definition of an Alabama atheist was somebody who didn't believe in Bear Bryant. The more literate football fans would talk about St. Aquinas' five proofs for Bryant's existence. You could ask someone if he'd heard that Bryant was in the hospital with a broken leg and when he said, no, he hadn't heard, you could tell him that it just came over the radio. Bryant had been out walking his pet duck when he got run over by a speedboat.

Nobody, of course, really believed in Bryant's divinity. If someone had been found preaching on a Birmingham street corner that Bear Bryant was God, however, he probably wouldn't have been considered what they call in Alabama, "locking-up crazy." Only a little quaint, or a touch under the weather.

But people in Alabama, serious people, did revere the man with a passion that remains hard for outsiders to believe and that recalls, more than anything, the affection that many Southerners, especially those who served under him, felt for Robert E. Lee. They believed in their leader with a devotion that was both touching and frightening.

There is the story of the occasion when the Confederate Army was camped out between marches, on the way to Gettysburg, and the men had stacked arms and were sitting around their campfires, talking. There was a British army observer along and he was telling the men around one of the campfires about Darwin's discoveries and his new theories about evolution. One fierce butternut listened for a while to the British officer's explanations and the arguments that followed. Finally, he spoke up. "Well, sir, *you* may be descended of an ape. And *I* certainly may be descended of an ape. But *General Lee* aren't descended of no ape."

In Alabama, Bryant's devoted followers would not allow questions about his competence or slurs on his honor. When he was accused of conspiring to fix a football game, Bryant filed a lawsuit and also went on statewide television to defend himself. Probably there was no need. Everyone in the state knew that it was just another case of the Yankee press smearing the South. But it was important for the football coach to go on television because he was the largest figure in the state and he had been slandered. Only the governor would have done the same thing. Bryant was equal to the governor in stature without having to go out and campaign every four years. His authority was of a more royal nature.

So, it comes as a surprise to some that he was not born in Alabama and that he did not spend his entire life there. He came from Arkansas. Moro Bottom, near Fordyce. The baby in a family of poor farmers who sold vegetables off the back of their wagon to make a little extra. He grew up knowing about mules and hard work. He was big, he had a temper, and he could fight.

Paul Bear Bryant. He won the lifetime nickname—you knew that he had become a national icon when the quotation marks no longer bracketed it—by going into the ring with a carnival bear to win five dollars, which was big money to a poor country boy in those times. He did it on a dare. Won, but never saw the money, the way he told the story. The name stuck, but you almost have to think it would have come to him some other way, if he'd never happened on that particular carnival and taken that specific challenge. He looked like a bear and, by the end of his career, when he had mastered a rumbling, rolling manner of speech that even good mimics had trouble imitating, he *sounded* the way a bear would sound, if a bear ever gave interviews and talked about football.

He went to the University of Alabama on a football scholarship in 1931. He played end, both ways. He was good but, early in his time at Alabama, he almost quit. An assistant coach named Hank Crisp, who was as much a legend in his time as Ken Donahue became in his, shamed him out of it. On another occasion, someone from the University had to call his uncle back in Arkansas and say, "Come get him. He keeps fighting everybody and we can't control him. So come get him."

According to the story, the uncle came to Tuscaloosa and had a talk with him. "Now Paul," he is supposed to have said, "if you don't stop this fighting, you're going to have to come back to Moro Bottom and get back behind those mules. You don't want that, do you?"

Bear stayed.

The football team he played for was one of the best that Alabama ever fielded. The stars of the team were Dixie Howell and Don Hutson, who later went on to the pros and set pass receiving records that stand today. Bryant did not have their kind of talent. He was routinely referred to as "the other end." But he had the kind of determination that showed so dramatically later on. He played one game with a broken leg and is supposed to have said afterwards that it wasn't much, there was only *one* broken bone.

In 1935, Alabama went to the Rose Bowl for the fourth time and beat Stanford 29–13. A small trivial footnote to the game is the fact that Ronald Reagan covered it as a reporter and the coach of the Alabama team, Frank Thomas, had been the Notre Dame roommate of the man who was to give Reagan his most celebrated movie role—George Gipp. Almost half a century later Reagan, as President, would give a Washington dinner to honor "the other end."

After he graduated, Bryant stayed in Tuscaloosa, married, and took a job as an assistant football coach. He had moved on to Vanderbilt four years later and then, after the Japanese bombed Pearl Harbor, he joined the navy.

They tell a story of how Bryant went around to colleges in the South recruiting young men for the navy flight program. He would stand up on the stage of the school auditorium and make his pitch, striking and formidable in his blues with the gold braid. At Sewanee, after he made his speech, several of the boys came up to talk to him. One was almost Bryant's size, a star on the football team. He said he wanted to join up. Bryant looked him up and down with the cold eye that he always saved for those with the greatest physical gifts and the most natural talent.

"Well," he said finally, "it looks to me like you're going to have to lose a few pounds first, fat boy."

Bryant's duties during the war usually had something to do with athletics—designing and administering conditioning programs for student aviators. But it was never likely that a man of such remarkable gifts for leadership would serve as a trainer for the entire war.

When his commanding officer began having troubles

with one of those allied operations that included, among others, some Free French forces in North Africa, he turned in desperation to Bryant. He and Bryant had become friends talking about football. They had both played. Bryant, of course, at Alabama and his commanding officer at the Naval Academy.

Finally, when the French had pushed the U.S. Navy to the limit of its patience, Bryant was called in. He was to be in charge, but because he had no command experience, his orders were written to cover everyone's tracks. According to the official language, his paramount duties were as base athletic officer with collateral duties as officer in charge. He was to take whatever steps were necessary to bring those Frenchmen into line. All copies of those orders were destroyed.

The French loved Bryant. Through the sheer force of his personality, he made them forget their bickering and cooperate with their allies. "No one ever knew quite how he did it," says the man who had those strange orders drafted. "But Bryant had a way of making you want to do what he wanted you to do. And he could make you think it was your idea."

The admiral in charge of that area of operations was immediately satisfied which, in turn, made the old Academy football player's life, and naval career, that much easier. Bryant returned to the States and was stationed at the University of North Carolina's pre-flight school. The school had a football team and Bryant was the head coach. Like many other young American men, the war had given him the opportunity he wanted, ten years earlier than he could have expected it. But Bryant was not content with mere good fortune and the title "Head Coach." He wanted some good football players and was not willing to trust chance, or normal navy channels, to supply them.

So Bryant went to see the man who had written those strange orders, detailing him to Agadir to handle the uncooperative French. Bryant arrived bearing a ten-pound ham and a small request. He would appreciate it, he said, if those potential aviators who had played some football could be sent to North Carolina instead of to some other base.

The commander was happy to accept the ham and to fulfill what seemed like a reasonable request. When the ballplayers began arriving at North Carolina, Bryant wanted the commander to know he appreciated it and wanted it to continue. This time, the ham weighed fifty pounds.

When the war ended, Bryant took a number of those players at North Carolina pre-flight with him to Maryland, where he had been given his first civilian head coaching opportunity. And those players helped him win there, too.

The officer who drew up the orders sending Bryant into battle with the French and then later sent those football players to him at North Carolina remained in the navy and eventually made admiral. By this time, Bryant was winning at Alabama. The admiral invited him to Pensacola, where he awarded Bryant an honorary set of old aviator's wings.

"Coach Bryant was a genius," he said. "He was a winner on and off the playing field because people wanted to do what Paul Bryant wanted them to do. Hell, I'd have sent those football players to him, ham or no ham, after the way he handled those Frenchmen."

Bryant's career as a head coach in college was stormy from the beginning. He seemed to know that what had worked for him in the navy would not work in civilian life. Where he had been a diplomat, practicing accommodation and flattery, before, he became an autocrat now, unwilling to share power or compromise. He left Maryland after one (winning) season, because the president of the University overruled him after he suspended a player from the team for disciplinary reasons.

Bryant went to Kentucky, a football also-ran, and built a winner. He took Kentucky to bowl games, among them the 1951 Sugar Bowl, where he accomplished a spectacular upset of an undefeated Oklahoma squad coached by Bud Wilkenson. Bryant coached players like George Blanda and Babe Parelli at Kentucky. In those days he relied on iron discipline and fear to motivate his players. George Blanda said much later that the first time that Bryant walked into a room, "I thought to myself that this must be what God looks like."

Though he won football games and brought great players to Kentucky in his eight seasons there, Bryant left the school in unfriendly fashion. Kentucky was a basketball school and the domain of Coach Adolph Rupp, who was called "Baron," and deserved his nickname every bit as much as Bryant deserved his. Bryant could not abide playing second fiddle to Rupp, said as much, and quit.

From Kentucky, he went to Texas A&M. It was there that his legend began to assume real shape and heft.

At Texas A&M, Bryant pushed his belief in sacrifice, hardship, and discipline to the limit. To many, he went beyond the limit and practiced "brutality," which was a word that followed him for a long time after A&M and was only dropped as he became a sort of avuncular folk hero to writers and broadcasters too young to remember the story of Junction City. . . .

Bryant inherited a losing program at A&M. Not having any quality football players to work with was his first problem. His second was more serious. Namely, it was difficult, if not impossible, to get any quality ballplayers from the state of Texas to come to A&M. The school was all-male, run on military lines, with the students called cadets and wearing uniforms. A&M was located out in the plains, in a desolate Texas town called College Station, the sort of place where the wives of new professors would take one look and weep. Asked to choose among, say, Texas, Oklahoma, SMU, and A&M, a high school star would find one aspect of the decision easy. He could narrow his choices to three schools, automatically. No one wanted to go to A&M. Bryant tried to recruit Don Meredith, who wanted to play for him, perhaps because he recognized what Bryant had done with his quarterbacks at Kentucky. But Meredith finally had to tell Bryant that if it were *anyplace* but A&M, there wouldn't be any question, but as it was . . . well, he was going to SMU.

So on the first day of September 1954, before his first season as coach of the Texas A&M Aggies, Bryant took the players he had and left College Station for an even bleaker place by the name of Junction City. They would hold their practices away from the dubious distractions of the campus.

The players lived in World War II quonset huts and they practiced on a grassless and shadeless field under a broiling Texas sun. The temperature was routinely over one hundred. For ten straight days, Bryant put the players through three practices a day. They quit in bunches. Years later, one of the men who survived said, "I can tell you how tough it was. When we went up there, it took two buses to carry us. When we came back, we couldn't even fill one."

Ninety-six players went to Junction City and all but 27 quit. And one of them had suffered a serious heat stroke that kept him out of several games. In football circles, those survivors are still held in the kind of awe that soldiers might save for men who lived through some terrible battle. One of them, Jack Pardee, remembers going out at five in the morning when it was still cool and practicing until eight or so when the heat began to rise. Then there would be meetings for an hour or two and another session that would start at ten or eleven in the morning. A final practice took place at three in the afternoon when the heat was at its peak. That practice lasted four hours, and by time to quit it would be getting dark.

All practices were in full pads with plenty of contact and no water. "You couldn't have any water, back then," Pardee says. "If you had to have water, then that meant you didn't have any discipline." Pardee is now a head coach in the United States Football League. He played professional football for the Rams and the Redskins and was known as a very tough, dedicated linebacker who, as the saying goes, "liked contact." He was operated on, during one off-season, for a cancer that is frequently mortal. He came back the next year.

Of Junction City, Pardee says, "You couldn't do that

again. If you tried it now, *everyone* would quit. I wasn't
going to quit because the only place I could go was back
to the oil fields and that didn't seem any better than football, even the way Bryant played it."

One of the legacies of Junction City is that it could not
happen again. The story got around and public reaction
to the brutality of the camp was such that off-campus
practices were made illegal by the NCAA.

Bryant's first year was dismal enough to make one wonder why he bothered. Who would imitate his methods if
they got you a record of 1–9?

Bryant himself later thought that he might have gone
too far at Junction City. "If I'd been one of the players,"
he said, "I might have quit."

Pardee thinks there might be something to that. "We
lost some games that we might have won if some of the
people who had a little talent hadn't quit during those
days at Junction. So I think he went a little too far."

But if he went too far at Junction City and suffered
through his first and only losing season as a head coach,
Bryant did turn A&M around. He was winning in his second year and undefeated in his third. If he was never quite
so tough again as he had been at Junction, he never turned
anything like soft. "He was tough the whole time," Pardee
says. "But he got some players to go with the philosophy.
Charlie Krueger. John David Crow. Real quality players.
And he had all of us believing if you worked hard, prepared,
gave it your very best . . . then good things would happen.
We trusted him."

Bryant's methods worked, then, at Texas A&M. Countless hairs were split in the press, and elsewhere, trying to
resolve the question—did Bryant preach, and practice,
brutal football? If he'd lost, there probably would have
been no debate. But he didn't and the answer to the question became "No, Bryant didn't teach brutality, he taught
winning."

The Junction City methods worked for Bryant. The discipline became the bond his teams needed. The history of
football is full of games where the better team beat the

team with the better players. This is one of the appeals of
the game. *Esprit* counts for something. It is an emotional
game and often just being good is not good enough. You
have to be good and you have to be hungry and you have
to play for the good of the team.

Shared sacrifice and hardship will bond football players
the same way it will bond soldiers. The greater the hardship, the stronger the bond. The survivors of Junction City
had been through something together that separated them
from everyone else. Surviving that together helped them
go on and win together—especially when Bryant had recruited some quality players. They were like the men of
Stonewall Jackson's brigade—marched like no infantry-
men had ever been marched before. But through the suffering, the brigade conquered, defeating three different
Federal Armies in the Shenandoah Valley campaign. "All
old Jackson gave us was a musket, a hundred rounds, and
a gum blanket," one of his veterans said. "Then he druv
us like hell."

Football may be a team sport, but as its deep students
always say, "it is a coaches' game." There is probably not
another sport in the world where coaching is so important.
A baseball manager might lose a few games or even win
one or two, because of his tactical skill or lack of it, but
90 percent of the time, the team could perform just as well
without him. A basketball coach can make a difference to
a team and several have. But one strong-shooting seven-
footer will do more for most losing teams than a coaching
change.

Football, however, is different. The team is the extension
of the coaches' will and intelligence. There are countless
coaches who have lost with great players and there are a
few who have won with ordinary players. This is the kind
of coach Bryant was. The line that captured that quality
about him was uttered by one of his assistants, Bum Phillips, who went on to become a successful head coach in
the pros. "Bryant can take his and beat yours," Phillips
said, "and then he can turn around and take yours and
beat his."

And, finally, Junction City worked for Bryant at A&M because football is a physical game, and the team that is toughest and best able to endure has a better chance of winning. This was even more of a consideration thirty years ago than it is now.

In those days, they played one-platoon football with very few substitutions. Bryant called it "Eleven Men and Sic 'Em," and he always preferred it to two-platoon football. A man who played had to expect to play every down unless he was injured. Coaches like Bryant loved that game because it put a premium on toughness and conditioning. In a game that was still undecided in the fourth quarter, the team that was in the best shape would win. Bryant's team, after the Junction City sort of practices, would find a game almost easy by comparison. They would be strong and getting stronger in the fourth quarter. Thirty years later Jack Pardee remembers a game against Rice when A&M was losing 13–0 with two minutes remaining. "We knew we could win it. We'd learned that from him and we believed it. And we were still strong. We scored three touchdowns and won 21–13."

So Bryant won at A&M and his reputation grew. But it wasn't an untainted reputation. There was the brutality business and, also, the fact that A&M was put on probation for recruiting violations while he was there.

Bryant maintained that he never paid players, though he knew they were being paid by rich alumni. At the time, the illegal recruiting methods merely seemed part of a piece, logically consistent with his obsession for winning.

Being put on probation was, in fact, a deep wound that Bryant never really got over. It cost his team a chance to appear in the Cotton Bowl the year they won the conference championship and were undefeated.

The year after A&M was banned from the Cotton Bowl, the team started out as though it intended to wipe out the memory of that season. A&M won its first seven games and was on its way to another undefeated season that, this time, would be properly concluded with a bowl appearance. Perhaps even a national championship.

But, as before in Bryant's career, not all the action was on the playing field or even on the practice field. There were other factors influencing his fortune, and the fortune of his players.

Alabama had been losing, dreadfully, while Bryant was winning at A&M. Losing, in Bryant's undefeated year, every single game it played. And, the year before that, losing all but two. The team had become the doormat of the conference and, to add to the humiliation, Auburn meanwhile had built itself into a national power. Something had to be done. Influential Alabama supporters had been lobbying for Bryant since his days at Kentucky and, now that he'd done well at A&M, with a program that was in worse shape than the one at Tuscaloosa, the pressure became more and more intense. Delegations were sent to Texas to speak to Bryant. Rumors circulated. The papers printed titillating stories promising that deliverance, in the shape of a bear, was on the way.

Bryant accepted Alabama's entreaties. He asked to be let out of the six years that remained on his ten-year contract with A&M so he could sign a similar contract with Alabama. When word leaked, his players became so demoralized that they lost their last three regular season games and instead of the Cotton Bowl, settled for the Gator Bowl, which they also lost.

Bryant's detractors were quick to point out that he seemed unable to hold himself to the same standards of dedication and commitment that he expected—no, *demanded*—from his players. They were expected to give their all for A&M. He would too . . . until he got a better offer.

Bryant's explanation for why he left A&M seemed mawkish and transparently insincere at the time. It was not for another fifteen or twenty years that anyone who was not intimate with him would ever believe that there was actually a sentimental side to the man. "I left Texas A&M because my school called me," he said at the time. "Mama called, and when Mama calls, then you just have to come running."

Someone with a more cynical view said of the move,

"Bryant will have Alabama winning in his first season, he'll make 'em national champions in his second, and he'll have 'em on probation in his third."

There was joy in Tuscaloosa when Bryant arrived. Some people took to saying he had "returned," as though he were another MacArthur come back as a liberator. Most fans were content to say that he'd "come home."

In Bryant's first season, 1958, the team won five games, lost four, and tied one. When he met with the freshmen, many of whom had been recruited by his assistants while he was still at A&M, he said, "I want to know why you're here. I want each one of you to ask himself what he's doing here. And I want you to know that if you're not here to win the national championship, then you don't belong here."

Alabama lost to Auburn in Bryant's first year at Alabama. The score was 14–8. The year before, it had been 40–0 and Auburn had finished the year as national champion. In Bryant's second year, Alabama beat Auburn and six other teams, tied two, and went to a bowl game for the first time in six years, losing the first Liberty Bowl to Penn State by 7–0.

In the next season, when those freshmen he'd challenged to win the national championship were juniors, Bryant's team won eight games and tied Texas in the Bluebonnet Bowl. They lost only one game, to Tennessee.

In 1961, his fourth season, those freshmen were seniors and Bryant was ready to take them all the way.

They beat Georgia in a hot opener. And they beat Tennessee. Beat them badly. 34–3. Coming down to the last two games in the schedule, Alabama was undefeated but had to beat Georgia Tech and Auburn to stay that way. Tech was always tough in those days.

Alabama won 10–0. It was such a convincing win that the final score became almost a footnote to the game. One play from that game took on symbolic proportions for Bryant, Alabama, and all of college football.

It happened on a punt. Alabama was coming downfield to cover when the Tech man signaled for a fair catch. One of his would-be blockers dropped his hands and relaxed just as an Alabama man reached that part of the field and hit him. It was basic football. Aggressive but not unusually so. When you go down to cover a punt, you look for someone to hit. Knock a man down and he can't block. Bryant taught it and his players learned what Bryant taught or they weren't his players very long.

On this occasion, perhaps because the Tech man had relaxed, the hit was more than "good contact." The Alabama player hit the Tech player in the head with his forearm, breaking his jaw. An official saw the play and did not call a penalty. The Tech player was carried off the field. After the game, Alabama coaches asked about him. The Tech coaches told them what they knew. Nobody seemed to think, at that time, that it was anything more than one of those things, the price of hard-hitting football, something coaches and players all know about.

But . . . that play became the kernel out of which grew a scandal and a lawsuit and a crisis in Bear Bryant's career.

The injured player was "Chick" Granning, who was a favorite with the fans and the press because he had the gifts to be an All-American but had been dogged by bad luck and tragedy. He was injured before the incident and had missed games when he might have starred. And then, on the night he was married, as he was driving off on his honeymoon, there was a wreck and his wife was killed.

And now, this injury.

The Alabama player who hit him was Darwin Holt. He was a defensive specialist. College football players still went both ways then, but whenever the ball changed hands, each team was allowed one substitution. This was the "wild card rule" and, at Alabama, the wild card was Holt, who came in for the quarterback when Alabama played defense.

Holt was one of Bryant's "little" boys. Some games he did not weigh 170 pounds. He was from East Texas, had gone to A&M to play for Bryant and, when Bryant left for Alabama, Holt had followed him there, giving up a year of his eligibility when he transferred and spending the extra year earning his master's degree.

Holt's name came over the stadium speaker several times every game. "Now playing for Alabama, at linebacker . . . Darwin Holt." The fans would cheer because Alabama was a defensive team—shutting out six teams that year, five of them consecutively—and, the thinking seemed to be that if you were a defensive specialist on a defensive team, then you were some special kind of tough. Alabama fans said that the NCAA was going to come up with a new penalty for unnecessary roughness—fifteen yards for "Holting."

"Darwin was just a dedicated player," one of his teammates remembers. "But he wasn't a dirty player, and I'll tell you why. Because Coach didn't want any dirty players. I remember when one boy got two fifteen yarders called on him in one game, Coach jerked him out of there so fast you wouldn't believe it. Over on the sideline he told him to sit down and that he'd be lucky if he ever played another down. 'You couldn't play four years and be good enough to cost the University of Alabama thirty yards,' he said. He was really hot. And he'd have done the same to Darwin if he'd played dirty. So he didn't play dirty, believe me."

Just the same, Holt's undeserved reputation as a headhunter, and the natural sympathy people felt for Granning, combined with sensational newspaper coverage, turned the incident into something much larger than anyone could have imagined at the time. It started in the days just after the Tech game and reached a crisis months later.

Before that, however, there was the Auburn game with the number one ranking on the line. The closest Bryant had come yet to that pinnacle in fifteen years as a head football coach. The game was a blowout, 34–0.

The 1961 Alabama team won the national championship. It also won the Sugar Bowl, beating Arkansas 10–3, which broke the string of shutouts, but made it seven games since anyone had scored a touchdown against Alabama. The team allowed only twenty-five points in eleven games. Auburn had driven to the three-yard line in the last regular season game. With first and three for the touchdown, one of the Alabama players had looked at the official and said, "You think these sumbitches are going to score?"

The official shrugged.

"Well, I'll tell you that they aren't."

They didn't. Someone said of that team that they took it personally when somebody scored on them.

It was Bryant's fourth team at Alabama. His first national championship. And, more than that, it was the team that best expressed whatever vision he had of football and the world. It was an almost perfect extension of him and all the drives and fears and gifts that had brought him this far through his often troubled 48 years in this vale of tears. It had not been easy and that, in an odd way, was how he seemed to like it.

Many people who knew Bryant well still say that the '61 team was the one that best represented him. Perhaps it is fairer to say that the '61 team best represented the *early* Bryant, for he seems to have had an uncommon ability to grow in a world that is more conservative than most. Through his thirty-two seasons, Bryant changed many times. He changed football tactics. He changed his thinking about training. He changed on haircuts when that was truly a *big* issue. He changed on race, though he might have been late there. The only thing he never seemed to change on was winning.

The '61 team featured some players who were almost emotional clones of Bryant in their desire to win football games, their willingness to work hard, sacrifice, and scratch and claw to do it. There was Holt, of course, who might not have played other places but who became a standout under Bryant. Billy Neighbors. Bobby Skelton. Billy Richardson.

Two players, however, seemed to sum up that team better than any of the others. One was Lee Roy Jordan and the other was Pat Trammell.

Jordan was a center/linebacker from Excel, a town so small that people who had lived in Alabama all their lives had never heard of it until the advent of Lee Roy Jordan. It is still true that hardly anyone in the state—even anyone

on the coaching staff at the University of Alabama—can
tell you where Excel is or how to get there. (It is a little
below Monroeville, which is where Harper Lee's novel *To
Kill a Mockingbird* takes place.) But everyone knows who
came from there. When he played football at Alabama,
Jordan went either by the name "Lee Roy," or by the
longer title of "Lee Roy Jordan from Excel, Alabama."

"I saw Coach tell Lee Roy to take off the pads and head
for the locker room a couple of times," one player remembers. "He wouldn't quit practicing and he couldn't practice
but one way . . . full out. He's got to be the only man who
ever *practiced* too hard for Coach Bryant."

He played like he practiced. He was a hard tackler who
was always around the ball, always in on the play, always
going full out. He was an All-American who went on to
play for the Dallas Cowboys for thirteen years. But Alabama people still think of him as the anchor of those teams
that expected to shut everyone out and, in '61, almost did.
They loved Lee Roy almost as much as Bryant, who would
sum up his feelings for Jordan by saying, "I'm not worried
about my defense because if they stay between the sidelines . . . then Lee Roy will get 'em."

The quarterback of the '61 team was Pat Trammell who,
given the line of quarterbacks that came out of the Bryant
stable, was no thoroughbred as an athlete. Bryant coached
Blanda and Parelli at Kentucky. Namath, Stabler, Sloan,
Richard Todd, Jeff Rutledge, and Walter Lewis at Alabama. But he was never as close to those quarterbacks as
he was to Trammell, who wasn't the athletic or artistic
equal of any of them.

Trammell was a doctor's son from Scottsboro who loved
to play and who could fight. Though he came from circumstances that Bryant would have considered prosper-
ous when he was growing up, Trammell had the same
combative streak. People liked to say that by the time he
came to Alabama, "Pat had whipped every man between
sixteen and sixty in the whole of Jackson County."

He is supposed to have stood up at the first meeting of
the freshmen players recruited during Bryant's first year

at Alabama, stuck a switchblade knife into the table and, while the blade still quivered, announced to everyone in the room that *he* was the quarterback.

He would fight his own teammates, on the field or back at the dormitory after practice if he thought they were not putting out one hundred percent. He would go whole games without calling a halfback's number for the same reason. He was not necessarily loved by his teammates, but he was their leader. He once quick kicked when Alabama was ahead and in relatively good field position. When he came to the sideline (Darwin Holt had come in for him to play defense) Bryant asked Trammell what was going on—why had he quick kicked?

"Well, they're not blocking anyone," he said, "so I thought I'd see if they could play defense."

Bryant considered no player his equal, especially not in those early, still-hungry days. But of all the players he dealt with, Trammell probably came the closest of any to being accepted by Bryant as something more than mere talent out there to do his bidding. Trammell could get away with what approached insubordination. In a fourth down situation, when the team was in the gray area where a field goal would be long and risky, a punt might put the other team in the hole, and a good play executed well might get the first down, Trammell looked to the bench for help. Nothing. No kicking team. No punter. He obviously thought this was the wrong strategy. So he put his hands on his hips and looked harder at the bench. Bryant turned away and busied himself with other matters. Trammell gave an elaborate, disgusted shrug and went back into the huddle to call the play. And he made the first down.

"Nobody else could have gotten away with that," one of his old teammates says. "Pat could do it, but anyone else, Coach would have skinned him alive."

He had a way, a gift for leadership and a love of the game, that made the romantics who followed Alabama football recall other heroes from other times. A woman from the state wrote a pretty good revisionist version of

King Arthur in which Trammell became Lancelot. And for historically minded fans, Trammell recalled the state's greatest Civil War hero, a young artillery officer named John Pelham, a mere major in 1863 but a hero of the Confederacy and a favorite of Lee's, who called him "The Gallant Pelham."

Historian Douglas Southall Freeman describes Pelham's career this way:

> The magnificent young commander of
> Stuart's Horse Artillery, the blond idol
> of many of the soldier-loving girls, goes
> on from splendor to splendor, makes
> peculiarly his own the title "gallant,"
> and on a March day, shouting "Forward"
> and smiling at troopers in a charge, he
> falls from his horse. Three girls in
> nearby towns put on mourning for him.

After the '61 national championships, Trammell graduated and went to Alabama medical school. There was never any chance he would play professional football. He didn't have the ability.

But he remained a hero in the state and all sorts of doctors in Birmingham were encouraging him to take up their specialties, hoping that he might eventually want to join in their practice after medical school, internship, and hospital residency. "Everybody wanted a piece of Pat," a man who has lived in Birmingham all his life remembers. "He was, truly, the golden boy."

Trammell had finished medical school when doctors found he had a rare form of lymphatic cancer. Bryant accompanied him to New York where he underwent surgery that, for several months, seemed to have succeeded. Then the cancer metastasized. Bryant saw Trammell in his hospital room, conscious, shortly before he died. He was 28.

Bryant said of him, when he was quarterback for the '61 national champions, "He can't run, he can't pass, and he can't kick—all he can do is beat you."

In the book *Bear*, which he wrote in collaboration with John Underwood, Bryant said, "There's never been a day since, that I didn't miss him."

The national championship had been Bryant's goal. Now he had achieved it. Nobody expected him to quit. Bryant had struggled all his life, it seemed, against the specter of poverty. He had a deep and very real fear of failing and having to return to the bottom land and those mules he remembered. This was no secret or unconscious fear, either. He admitted to it. He wanted success, he would say, because he knew all about the other thing.

So now he had his success. But it would be a while yet, many years and several crises, before he would be allowed to savor it.

In 1962, he had another fine team. Trammell had graduated, but Lee Roy was back for one last year. The team started out winning, right away, and won the first eight games. No team scored more than seven points against Alabama and Lee Roy. It was the same kind of tough defense that had carried Alabama all the way the year before. Alabama fans loved it.

But not everyone did. In October, the *Saturday Evening Post*, which was still in existence and still a publication of wide circulation and vast authority, ran a story called, "College Football Is Going Berserk." The article was by an Atlanta sportswriter who lamented the way college football had declined into brutality (which somebody had been lamenting, periodically, ever since Teddy Roosevelt had threatened to have the sport outlawed) and accused Bryant of being the primary influence. The Chick Granning incident was cited as proof that the trend existed and that Bryant was culpable.

The article was sensational and unfair—Alabama and Bryant wouldn't have been cited if they had just come off a five and four season—and probably would have passed into the oblivion that is saved for breathless magazine pieces if it had come at another time. But this was 1962.

John Kennedy had been elected President. During the campaign he had won votes—perhaps enough to insure his election—by writing a letter of support to Martin Luther King, Jr., who was serving time in an Alabama jail. Alabama had become a national symbol for the old, intransigent ways of Jim Crow. Alabama was the state where George Wallace would campaign on a platform of "Segregation Today; Segregation Tomorrow; Segregation Forever." A state where Bull Conner would turn the dogs and the fire hoses loose on demonstrators in Birmingham. Where protestors who had come to the state for the Selma march would be murdered at night, out on lonely back country roads. This was all before the northern cities rioted, so it was easy to hate Alabama then and to feel superior to the state, its people, and its agony. And easy, as well, to say that the Alabama football team won games because it played dirty.

Bryant sued over that story. His team also lost to Georgia Tech that year, 7–6. Alabama went for two, to win the game, and didn't make it. (The two-point conversion is to football what the *deus ex machina* is to formal drama.) But Alabama went on to play in the Orange Bowl against Oklahoma. The Oklahoma coach was Bud Wilkenson. Kennedy had appointed him head of the President's Council on Physical Fitness. He was one of those people pulled, as though by gravity, into the Kennedy orbit. He was thin and professorially handsome. He could speak unaccented, politically acceptable, inspirational phrases of the sort Kennedy liked. He fit right into Camelot and, before the Orange Bowl, Kennedy dropped by the Oklahoma dressing room to wish him and his team well.

The President had nothing to say to Alabama or to Bryant. Alabama won the game 17–0. Lee Roy Jordan made twenty-four tackles.

In the spring of 1963, the *Saturday Evening Post* published a second article about Bryant. This one accused him of conspiring to fix a football game which, if the charges held up, would have amounted to the greatest scandal in sports since Arnold Rothstein fixed the 1919 World Series.

This was the occasion when Bryant went on statewide television to denounce the story in which the *Post* claimed a man had picked up a phone and overheard Bryant talking with Wally Butts about how to fix the upcoming Georgia game. He filed suit and eventually settled out of court for almost half a million dollars. The story was thoroughly discredited. The plays that were described in the article did not exist. The technical football was thoroughly unsound and players as well as coaches testified to that fact. Bryant beat the *Saturday Evening Post* on that story as well as on the brutality story that had run earlier. That hapless magazine eventually went out of business and it is fair to say that the money paid to Bryant as a result of those two stories hastened its inevitable demise.

But it is worth noting that the *Saturday Evening Post* was a mass circulation weekly magazine, an American institution claiming to be the nation's oldest periodical. It had been founded by Ben Franklin, no less. In those days of relative innocence before Vietnam and before Watergate, no magazine like the *Saturday Evening Post* would have gone after a figure like Bear Bryant unless he was vulnerable. Bryant may have won his national championship in 1961—and another in '64, followed by one more in '65—but to many he was still an outlaw. Still the sort about whom it could be said, in good circles, "He teaches brutality," and even, "He fixes games."

Which made the people in Alabama love him that much more.

In the sixties, especially the early sixties, the people of Alabama embraced Bear Bryant as the one true coach. His faith was their faith. He could take little white boys from the farms and make them into a team that could take on anyone, including the team that had the blessing of President Kennedy, and whip them straight up. He could beat the national press when it said that he taught dirty football and/or that he cheated. He could even, in 1966, take his team of little boys from the most despised state in the union to the Sugar Bowl and beat a team of bigger, stronger boys from Nebraska, some of them black, and finish as the only undefeated school in the whole country and then still not get the national championship because *everyone was against him . . . and us.*

If there is anything more satisfying than being the best, it is being the best and despised for it. Bryant and Alabama football were, therefore, on top of the world in 1967.

Then things started going bad for the Bear. Alabama was tied by Florida State in its first game of the 1967 season. Being tied was bad enough, but the score made it worse. 37–37. More points given up in one game than were scored on the '61 national champions all season. Where was Lee Roy? Bryant actually turned to an assistant during that game and told him to get Lee Roy and put him in the game. The coach said, "I just went and hid. I sure wasn't going to be the one to tell him Lee Roy had graduated four years ago." The '67 team also lost to Tennessee. The first time that had happened since 1960. Then Alabama went to the Cotton Bowl and lost to Texas A&M, which was coached by Gene Stallings, who had been one of the A&M players to survive Junction City under Bryant. It was one of the rare occasions when Bryant lost to one of his former players or assistants.

The next year the team lost three games, including a 35–10 embarrassment to Missouri in the Gator Bowl. Alabama was not even in one of the major New Year's Day bowls that year. There was also a second straight loss to Tennessee to chew on.

The year of 1969 was the worst yet. Five defeats. Another to Tennessee. And the first loss to Auburn since 1963. A loss to Colorado in the Liberty Bowl. Merely going to the Liberty Bowl left a taste of humiliation in the mouth of any loyal Alabama fan. To lose there was enough to make the faithful gag.

The 1969 team gave up 268 points in eleven games. The '61 national champions, anchored by Lee Roy, had given up 25.

Unlikely as it might have seemed, 1970 started out as if it could be even worse. And in many ways, perhaps it was.

The first game Alabama played was in Birmingham, against Southern California. Bryant was still playing little white boys. A big black fullback named Sam Cunningham ran all over them. "They scored 42 points," Bryant said, "but it could have easily been a hundred." 1965 seemed a long time ago.

Tennessee beat Alabama for the fourth straight year. After the game, a Tennessee linebacker said to an Alabama assistant, "I don't know what the problem with your boys is, Coach. But it doesn't seem like that red jersey means much to 'em anymore." The pure bitter gall . . . to hear that from a Tennessee player, after you have just lost 24–0. Auburn, inevitably, beat Alabama and then, after an uninspired tie in the Bluebonnet Bowl (*Bluebonnet Bowl?*) the record for the year was 6–5–1. The defense had given up 264 points.

Auburn was highly ranked. Pat Sullivan was considered a red-hot candidate for the Heisman the next year and a certain All-American, along with his favorite pass catcher Terry Beasley. They had both been recruited by Alabama . . . both had chosen Auburn instead, and they had beaten Alabama two years running.

The NCAA had voted Bryant the Coach of the Decade one year earlier. Alabama had the best record of any major college during the sixties—90–16–4. But in 1970, that glory seemed part of the long ago. Alabama was now a mediocre team, second best in the state, and going to inferior bowls on the strength of its name, not its record. And losing in those games, as well.

There were rumors about Bryant. That he was ill. Drinking. Considering retirement. Another job. Someone who could claim to know, because he had talked to someone in Tuscaloosa who knew Bryant's banker, would say that he'd heard that Bryant had been out on a yacht in the Atlantic, before the last Orange Bowl he went to, and he'd put his feet up on the railing, taken a taste of Johnny Walker Red, and said "Well, this is it. The hard times are all behind me."

Somebody else had heard it on unimpeachable authority that Bryant was going to leave Alabama and college football and move up to the pros. He'd been offered a package that included a piece of the team—how could he turn it down, a man who liked money as much as the Bear? The University couldn't pay him any real money. He always got paid a dollar less than the president of the University. There were probably assistant coaches in the pros making that kind of money. No telling what he'd bring home if he was head coach, general manager, *and* had a piece of the team. And, anyway, he'd done everything he could do in college ball and he was a restless man. Look how much moving he'd done already in his life. He was a man who needed a challenge and there wasn't any left for him in college ball now. He'd done it all.

Bryant helped the rumors along by grumbling that the athletic director was getting pretty unhappy with the job the head coach was doing and that if things didn't change soon, then the athletic director might just find it necessary to fire the head coach. Bryant was, of course, both head coach and athletic director.

The truth seems to have been that he *was* bored, a little, and that he *was* considering an opportunity in the pros. Also, the game, along with society, had changed. The old Junction City methods did not work any longer. This was the time of Vietnam and the military was being held in as low regard as the military-style methods of coaches like Bryant, who had lived through the Depression and the Second World War and had been indelibly influenced by those times.

The race question had long since been settled, at least as an abstract issue. Segregation was dead. Alabama, like the rest of the country, would eventually integrate. All-white football teams were relics, embarrassments, and losers. For every measure of satisfaction the racists had taken from the 1966 Orange Bowl, Sam Cunningham paid them back double in Birmingham when he ran for more than two hundred yards against white Alabama players who simply could not stop him.

So there were external changes that had an effect. But

the man himself had changed, as well. Bryant was bored enough to consider what would be called, today, a career change. Perhaps he was even in the throes of a mid-life crisis, though the phrase seems absolutely inappropriate when applied to someone as apparently lacking in introspection or self-pity as Bryant.

Nonetheless, he was considering a job offer. Head coach of the Miami Dolphins. A contract that was both long and fat. The absolute end of money worries for a man who had been acutely, painfully, obsessively worried about money ever since he could remember. Negotiations had gone far enough that a contract had been drawn up in Miami, meeting all of his terms, and sent to him in Tuscaloosa, where he sat on it and brooded.

He came to a decision at his friend Jimmy Hinton's house. Hinton is a very shrewd businessman and poker player who got Bryant into some things that made him a lot of money, among them a meat packing operation and something that Hinton calls, euphemistically, a "little lumber business," which was actually a plant that made ammunition boxes for the army, which during the Vietnam War could not produce enough. Before he went in with Hinton, Bryant had a very uneven investment record. Hinton helped make him rich. Hinton approached business and money the way Bryant approached football.

Bryant had the contract from the Dolphins in his coat pocket when he sat down one night to dinner at Hinton's house. He still could not make up his mind.

Hinton says, "I told him he didn't need to go down there, where he didn't know anybody, just to make money and meet a challenge. He had a challenge where he was. He could make plenty of money here. And this was where his friends were and his family wanted to be. I don't believe I told him anything he wasn't already thinking. But it might have helped for him to hear it from somebody else."

So Bryant decided to stay in college football, stay in Tuscaloosa, and start doing again what he had done before—winning.

"We had a meeting," Dude Hennessey, one of Bryant's

assistants at Alabama, remembers, "and Coach just said that people hadn't been doing the job they were paid to do. And that included him. But that it was going to stop. Anyone who couldn't produce, and do what he was being paid to do, was going to be out the door. And that included him, too. He told us he'd fire any one of us that he decided wasn't doing the job. And he told us he'd fire himself if he decided he wasn't doing the job. Then we all went out and started doing the damned job."

The 1971 team opened against USC on the West Coast. Southern Cal was expected to be very good, a contender for the national championship. The kindest thing anyone had to say about Alabama was that it was "rebuilding."

Bryant had made two changes in the off-season. First, he had started recruiting black ball players. "Sam Cunningham," people often said, "did more for integration in Alabama in two hours than Martin Luther King, Jr., did in ten years."

The first black man for Alabama was a man named John Mitchell, who was from Mobile but had been playing for two years at a junior college in Arizona. All sorts of major colleges were after him. "I could have gone to Notre Dame. I was planning on going to Southern Cal when Alabama started recruiting me. I was like every football player who grows up in Alabama . . . I wanted to play for Coach Bryant. I didn't think I would ever have the chance because I was black."

Bryant warned Mitchell and his parents that it wouldn't be easy for him at Alabama, but that he would do everything he could so that it wouldn't be too hard. Mitchell says, "He asked me, if I had a problem, if I would always come talk to him about it first, before I went to the press. That's all he asked from me.

"I came in during Christmas break and they put me in a dormitory room. All the other players were still at home. My roommate, who was white, walked in and saw me and I don't think anyone had told him. He tried not to let on, but he had this look on his face. But he introduced himself and that was that. We're still friends. Talk every week."

Mitchell played first team defense and, in his senior year, after he'd played "a really bad game," Bryant sent for him.

"I told him I'd been thinking about quitting," Mitchell remembers. "He looked at me and said, 'The first time you quit, it's hard. And the second time, it gets easier. And the third time, you don't even have to think about it.' Then he told me I wasn't a quitter and he'd see me at practice. But he moved me down to the second team and I stayed there for about a week. One game. And that really got my attention."

Mitchell took some abuse, which was to be expected. "Probably Jackson, Mississippi, was the worst place. They got on me pretty good there." But nothing from his own teammates. And he says that he would do it again, "in a minute. If you're a football player, you dream of playing for Coach Bryant."

The other change did not carry any vast sociological implications. It was a matter of football tactics and hence, a tightly kept secret. Bryant didn't care who knew he was recruiting blacks—he wanted it known, in fact—but he didn't want anyone to know that his offense was going to run out of the wishbone in 1971.

He had decided that the formation was the answer to his lack of passing and pass-catching talent. The wishbone relies on running, good fakes, and sound line play. Those things can be taught by good coaches and mastered by dedicated players. Which made it just right for Alabama and Bryant. So the Coach learned the fundamentals from his friend Darrell Royal, the head coach at Texas, where the wishbone had first appeared. Then he went back to Tuscaloosa and taught it to his team in great secrecy. The lid stayed on until the Alabama offense took the field for the first time against USC. Bryant had even sent an assistant coach up into the radio booth, to make sure John Forney didn't say anything about the wishbone with only a few minutes left before the kickoff.

Alabama won the game 17–10. It was an astonishing upset that seemed less and less astonishing as the season

went on. Alabama was still undefeated when it came time
for the Auburn game. Auburn was also undefeated. Pat
Sullivan had been named winner of the Heisman trophy
a week before the game. The pre-game tension seemed, by
kickoff, to have reached some new level, and a kind of
contagious hysteria hung over the state. Either of these
teams could be number one. Auburn passed. Alabama ran.
They both played mean defense. There was, by God, going
to be a war in Birmingham.

Turned out it was one of those games that fell hopelessly
short of its billings. Alabama won 38–6. Then both Alabama and Auburn lost in bowl games. The virulent hysteria that had seized the whole state for two weeks before
the game seemed to have left both teams too weak and
lethargic to compete again that year.

But Alabama was most definitely back. As good as the
sixties had been, by sheer arithmetical comparison, the
seventies were even better. Alabama became the only school
ever to win more than 100 games during a decade. One
poll or another called Alabama the national champions in
three different years. In 1979, the team was undefeated,
untied, and number one according to all the major polls.
The year before, Alabama played Penn State in the Sugar
Bowl. Penn State was undefeated and Alabama had lost
once. The game was played for the national championship
and, because it was played in New Orleans, thousands of
Alabama people were in the stands. They saw the single
play, the one moment, that for many people summed up
Bryant's teams once and for all.

Alabama was ahead in the fourth quarter of a tough
defensive game, 14–7. But Penn State recovered an Alabama fumble inside the twenty, then drove to a first and
goal at the eight. A run picked up two yards, and then a
pass play looked like a certain touchdown, but an Alabama
back recovered and drove the receiver out of bounds at the
one. Penn State had two plays to go three feet and the
enclosed Superdome rocked. Less than seven minutes to
go. The number one team in the nation, behind by a touch-

down, and one yard out. If the red shirts could hold, then they would be number one.

On third down, Matt Suhey tried to go over the top and was met in mid-flight. He did not make it in and the Penn State quarterback called for a spot. The ball was ten inches from the end zone. He spread his hands that distance apart and signaled his bench. One foot.

"You got a foot to go," one of the Alabama linemen said. "So you'd better pass."

Penn State came out of the huddle and lined up over the ball. The Alabama line closed ranks so that their shoulders seemed to touch. The crowd had gone, by then, beyond delirium.

The ball was snapped. Fullback Mike Guman took a handoff and went up. At least three Alabama players met him on the way and stopped him an inch or two before he went over. One of the Alabama players was knocked unconscious. The force of the hit had cracked his helmet.

Among Alabama fans, it became known as the "greatest goal line stand ever." A vivid oil painting was done of the exact moment of impact. The numbered prints sold and sold and, for years, hung prominently in restaurants and bars around the state. You still see an awful lot of them, faded a little with age. But people coming in to have a drink or to eat still stop in front of those paintings and say, "You know, I was there and I saw it. That was the greatest goal line stand ever."

The teams in the seventies were not made up of little-bitty quick boys. They were made up of big, strong, quick boys. And lots of them. Bryant would play as many as three entire units in a game, and not only in the games that were runaways. He was deep enough in football talent that the second team offense, many years, was every bit as good as the first team offense. And the third team offense was *almost* as good. Bryant was a one-platoon football man at heart, but if platooning was the game, then he'd out-platoon everybody else. It wasn't "Eleven men and sic 'em," but it was still winning.

Alabama's were big, confident teams that won on ability and talent more than emotion and pride. They still had plenty of the latter, all winning football teams do, but it had often seemed like those teams of the early sixties had only that, that they won when they weren't supposed to because they just wouldn't lose. Those teams in the seventies were supposed to win, which they did. They beat everybody (except Notre Dame and Texas; Bryant never won a game against either school) and, as the number of victories climbed past two hundred and began to close in on three hundred, the dimensions of Bryant as a coach, a leader, and a man became apparent. He was no longer merely a tough, winning football coach in the eyes of the media or the world. He was a giant fast becoming a myth.

And the beauty of that—whether you were an Alabama fan or not—was that he deserved it. If he had quit and gone to the pros when he had the chance—or just retired, gotten out of football altogether—he would have been remembered as one of the good ones. As good as Bobby Dodd at Georgia Tech. Or Frank Howard at Clemson. Almost as good as Wilkenson of Oklahoma and Hayes of Ohio State.

But he stayed. And while he stayed and kept winning, all the others started getting out. Parseghian at Notre Dame quit, burned out by pressure from perhaps the only alums with higher expectations than those from Alabama. Parseghian had won three national titles at Notre Dame, but the broadcast booth looked friendlier than the practice field and the sidelines on game day. Darrell Royal of Texas quit. He said he just couldn't stand the indignity of recruiting high school boys anymore, that it just wasn't right that a grown man should have to beg a young boy like that. And furthermore, there was so much cheating. Royal was a friend of Bryant's and a Texas hero. Nobody, not even Bryant, could out-country-boy him. Royal's phrase for a tough, hard-hitting game was, "There was some snot knocking in the okra today." Asked once if he planned to do anything different in a big game his team was about to play, he spoke the immortal football lines, "No, we'll dance with the one that brung us." But he finally just had to quit coaching. Bryant, who was older than Royal, kept at it.

He kept at it after Woody Hayes had to quit when he made a mistake that recalled, in eerie fashion, the fate of his hero, General Patton. Hayes slugged a Clemson football player who had intercepted an Ohio State pass and run out of bounds in front of the outraged coach. Hayes and Bryant were also friends. Their teams had met only once. Alabama won, decisively, in the 1976 Sugar Bowl, 38–6.

John McKay quit coaching USC to go into the pros. Bobby Dodd, who had coached at Georgia Tech when Alabama and Tech played those close tough games and when Chick Granning's injury had launched a crisis, retired. Bud Wilkenson had quit much earlier and run for the Senate from Oklahoma and lost. Wilkenson held one of the few coaching records Bryant never challenged. Most consecutive victories: 57. Bryant had 28 once.

Bob Devaney, who had coached the Nebraska teams Bryant beat in the sixties, had quit years before. Also Duffy Daugherty, of Michigan State, who once said, "The alumni are with you win or tie."

They were all gone but Bryant. He was still at it. Beating teams that were coached by men who had played for him. He beat Steve Sloan when he was at Mississippi. He beat Bill Battle when he was at Tennessee. He beat Charlie McLendon when he was at LSU and, eventually, cost his one-time assistant his job. McLendon was one of the most popular coaches in the South—at least among other coaches and the press. When Shug Jordan heard that McLendon had been fired, when his record was one of the best in the conference, he asked a reporter, "What happened to old 'Charlie Mac'? Why'd they get rid of him?"

"I don't know, Coach. I guess it was because he couldn't beat Bryant."

"Hell," Jordan snorted. "Who can? You go by that and they'll have to fire us all."

All together, Bryant was 41–6 against men who had either played for him or worked for him as assistants. When he began to beat his old players and to recruit some

of their sons, it seemed to occur to people that there had
to be more to Bryant than mere toughness. The brutality
business—even if it had been true, or completely true—
never could have carried him this far. Other men had tried
to build football teams that way and failed. A former assistant of Bryant's named Charlie Bradshaw had gone to
the head coach job at Kentucky and tried to build a team
using the old Junction City methods. But it hadn't worked
and Bradshaw was gone quickly. To focus on the brutality
was to mistake a part for the whole.

It was also part of the legend that Bryant was *not* a great
innovator as a coach. Not an especially astute student of
the game, a watcher of film, a drawer of X's and O's on
the blackboard. Bryant liked to perpetuate this notion. He
didn't want people to think he was smart, which is the
oldest country boy trick in that very old book of theirs.

"Let me tell you about Coach and the X's and O's,"
Darwin Holt said once, with some heat, after he heard
someone say that Bryant wasn't especially good at that
part of the game.

It was the Georgia Tech game of 1960 when Alabama
came back after being down 15–0 at the half (an insur-
mountable lead, almost, in those days of tough defense).
Holt said, "Coach Bryant had come in and told everyone
how the second half was going to be ours and we had 'em
right where we wanted them. Everybody's confidence was
coming back and we were all set to go back out on the
field. Just as we were leaving the dressing room, he called
me and Lee Roy over and said he wanted to show us how
to play the second half. He got the clipboard and showed
us how their guards were pulling. What he wanted us to
do, he said, was cross key on the pulling guard. If the guard
in front of me pulled, I was supposed to go with him and
Lee Roy would loop around and come in through the hole
that guard left. If the guard in front of Lee Roy pulled, then
we'd do just the opposite. That was it. We went back out
there and Lee Roy and I, especially Lee Roy, spent the
whole second half in their backfield. They never did figure
it out. Coach didn't get the idea for that from somebody

else. So don't tell me he didn't know the X's and the O's. He knew the X's and the O's and then he knew a lot more, too."

While Bryant said, correctly, that he borrowed the wishbone from Darrell Royal and then went on about how he wasn't smart enough to think up something like that himself, Royal pointed out that nobody ever figured out a way to pass off that formation until Bryant started fooling around with it.

"Listen," one of his old players said, "he didn't win all those games by being dumb about football. If he wanted people to think he wasn't a great technical coach, then he had a reason. And most of those technical coaches are still trying to win their first hundred games and worrying about their jobs. Coach knew as much as he had to know. He knew enough to win."

All along, the line about how Bryant wasn't a great technical coach was really nothing more than a way of making the point that he was so much more than that. "He didn't coach football," the Bum Phillips line went, "he coached people." And that, finally, was the category where his genius showed most clearly: in the matter of leadership. Teaching, motivating, coaching, leading. That was what he did best—better than anyone.

Sports Illustrated's John Underwood has written about an occasion when, "Before an important road game one year, he invited me to live with the team to get the makings of a story. At the pregame breakfast on Saturday, I sat next to an Alabama professor who had been invited along. Bryant curried faculty support by doing things like that, itself a form of communication. When he made his talk to the team, he barely spoke above a whisper. The players leaned forward in their seats, and one tipped over a glass of water. The spill hitting the floor sounded like Niagara Falls. When Bryant finished, the professor turned to me, awed. 'If I could reach my students like that I'd teach for nothing,' he said."

Bryant, it should be said, probably could have reached that professor's students. A magazine writer now living in Birmingham remembers how, when he was a student at

Alabama, he attended a ceremony for some very bright high school students who were involved in a nationwide contest that involved computer models and high math. "They were the kind of kids who played Dungeons and Dragons and went on from there. Most of them were from California and New Jersey. The University held a ceremony and asked Bryant to be the guest speaker. Which seemed like a funny choice since he didn't know anything about computers and these kids didn't know anything about football.

"But he came in and started talking about the things he always talked about. Sacrifice and dedication and hard work. It was hard to hear because he was mumbling the way he did. But those kids were all leaning forward like they were hanging on every word. By the time he was finished he had them in his hand. They stood up and started cheering and applauding and he had a hard time getting out of there, so many of them wanted autographs. I'll bet a lot of those kids hadn't been so fired up and emotional before in their whole lives."

As the seventies drew down, this gift, along with the sheer awesome presence of the man, began to dawn even on those who were not great football fans. The reason for this was simple enough, Bryant was about to *break the record*. One of those marks that was thought beyond the reach of any mortal, the way Babe Ruth's career home run record of 714 was supposed to be beyond anyone's reach until Henry Aaron broke that record. Or Ty Cobb's career record of 4,191 hits was supposed to be forever invulnerable until Pete Rose, at 44, broke that record.

Bryant was going for 315 career victories. He would do it, if he stayed on schedule, sometime in 1981, and when he did it, he would break the record of Amos Alonzo Stagg, whose name was virtually synonymous with college football and who was born two years before the surrender at Appomattox. He had been a head coach for 57 years, with his best years coming at the University of Chicago and College of the Pacific, neither of which has played football in decades. Stagg retired when he was 91. When he died, in 1965, he was 103.

In 1980 Bryant, who had a born, nearly genetic sense of the theatrical, won his 300th game against Kentucky, the school where he might still have been coaching except for Adolph Rupp and basketball. When the 1981 season opened, and the schedule was studied, it looked like Bryant would win number 315 in Tuscaloosa, in the stadium named for him, where he had lost only one game since coming to Alabama.

It probably seemed fitting, but the drama turned out to be even better than that. Alabama lost an early season game to Georgia Tech and then was tied by Mississippi Southern. Now, if the record were to be broken that season, Alabama would need to win all the games remaining.

The team went to State College to play Penn State in November. Penn State was ranked fifth in the nation. This was the team that had been stopped in "the greatest goal line stand ever."

In 1981, it happened again. Penn State was behind but got an interference call that put the ball on the Alabama one. A score would put them back in the game. The Alabama defense stopped four straight running plays for no gain and when they came off the field, Bryant tipped his hat to each man on the squad. That game tied the record at 314. In two weeks, Bryant would go for the record, in Birmingham, against Auburn.

Could it be any better, if you lived in Alabama, than that?

It was a fine football day and both teams had, as they say, "come to play." Auburn had a new coach, Pat Dye, who had learned coaching from Bryant and, though he loved the man, he loved what he stood for more. He wanted to win, record or no. And Auburn took a 17–14 lead into the fourth quarter.

Then the Alabama offense drove the length of the field and scored on a pass play. It was one of those drives when a team looks unstoppable, when the stakes are much greater than one football game and the desire comes from tradition, history, roots, soil, and other things that football players seldom talk about. "We wanted to win it for *him*," one of the Alabama players said after the game, "and we knew we had to do it right then. It just had to be."

Alabama won the game: number 315. Bryant took calls from President Reagan and former President Carter. Vain and proud as anyone would have to be to accomplish what he had, Bryant also carried an honest streak of humility inside and on the occasion of the record, it showed.

"Sometimes," he said, "I wish they wouldn't keep records. You count the games because it's too hard to count the kids, the parents, the high school coaches, the preachers, everyone who has touched every kid. Multiply a whole lot of years by a whole lot of people and you've got three-hundred-and-some victories, and all of the bowls couldn't hold all of the people who hold the record."

So Bryant achieved, with 315, the only kind of immortality that he ever wanted and, though he seemed serene as he moved into mythical status, he was, in truth, a restless, bored, and sometimes tormented man. Too big and too driven, perhaps, to ever find peace.

"He was terribly restless in Tuscaloosa those last few years," a man who knew him well says. "It was as though the town was too small and too stifling for him. He was always leaving on trips. Sometimes it seemed like he couldn't wait to get away."

He loved to gamble and he had a special fondness for the Las Vegas crap tables. One night at one casino he made such loud protests about how much he had lost and how the house must have been cheating that he was actually asked to leave. "Coach, we love you here," the pit boss said, "but even you can't accuse us of cheating."

As he became a celebrity, he became friends with other celebrities, and he seemed to enjoy them and their company more than he liked being home in Alabama. He knew Frank Sinatra and he knew John Wayne. People who were at one of those celebrity dinners remember seeing John Wayne and Bear Bryant sitting on the same couch, both of them a little flushed with alcohol, and thinking that by God, *there* was a pair.

Later, when John Wayne died, one Alabama fan said, "Now who will they get to play Bryant when they make the movie?"

(One answer was George C. Scott because, as one fan said, "He got plenty of practice playing Patton." The actual solution was a very good actor named Gary Busey, who labored mightily in an awful, doomed effort called, simply, *Bear*.)

Bryant had rich friends and he would fly around the country with them in their private planes or stay with them in their magnificent homes. But it was not something he wanted known. When he fell and broke some ribs in a friend's Palm Beach house, he refused to go to the hospital there. Instead, he flew back to Tuscaloosa where he put out the story that he'd hurt himself falling in the tub at home.

Bryant, who had always liked a drink, began to drink too much during this time. So much, on occasion, that he would admit himself to private hospitals to dry out. "It's just when I'm bored," he told John Underwood. He donated a substantial amount of money to one of the clinics where he'd been helped.

The symptoms were plain enough. Now that there were no more worlds to conquer, life did not hold all that it had once. He handled his sorrows with dignity and when his health began to fail—he had a stroke the year before he set the record—he kept it to himself. He understood his duties as a giant.

He was generous with his time and with his money. He would always find time for his old ballplayers who would drop in for visits. He helped them when he could. "He gave away thousands and thousands of dollars, a lot to his old players in business loans he never expected to collect," Jimmy Hinton says.

He could have made himself a dictator at the University

but a new president, Dr. Joab Thomas, arrived in 1981 and found him "the easiest head coach or athletic director to deal with in my experience." Thomas had been at North Carolina State and other universities before he came to Alabama and it was, he says, "with some trepidation that I called Coach Bryant in to speak to him, fairly early in my term, about a payroll matter."

Bryant listened and explained that what he was doing was perfectly legal. He had an assistant coach on half pay with the athletic department and half pay in alumni affairs, which enabled him to hire another, part-time coach on his budget.

"I told him," Thomas says, "Coach, I know it's legal but I don't think it looks right."

"And he said, 'Yes sir. I'll take care of it this afternoon.' "

As the 1982 season began, Bryant had no more records to shoot for. Every victory merely fattened his own record. He might win another national championship. People in Alabama assumed that this was his goal. To be number one, again, before he retired. He would reach the state's mandatory retirement age of seventy in two more seasons, but if he felt like staying . . . well, everyone was fairly certain the legislature could see its way clear to granting him an extension since anyone who voted against it would be committing certain political suicide.

Alabama started the 1982 season like contenders, winning five straight before losing to Tennessee for the first time in twelve years. Then, after two more wins, Alabama did something it had never done with Bryant as head coach. It lost three straight football games, including one in Tuscaloosa, and also the last and most important game of the season, the one against Auburn. Fans around the state were in something like shock.

The season was over and Alabama stood at 7–4. Not bad at most football universities, but intolerable there. The most distressing piece of evidence was the fact that the defense had allowed more than two hundred points. This had not happened since those two awful years, '69 and '70, when Bryant seemed ready to quit.

Around the state, people assumed that losing four games and giving up two hundred points would merely light a fire under Bryant once more. "Losing," he used to say, "just makes me get up earlier in the morning to find a way to beat you." Next year, he'd be some kind of tough.

Alf Van Hoose, the sports editor of the *Birmingham News*, was going down to visit a friend and do some fishing a week after the Auburn game. This was the time between regular season games and bowl games. Nothing but pro football and basketball to write about. Which makes it a slow time for Alabama sportswriters. College football is so completely the dominant sport in that state that the man who preceded Van Hoose, Benny Marshall, once called Vince Lombardi, "the poor man's Bear Bryant." Van Hoose decided to stop in Tuscaloosa, on the way to his fishing, to speak to the coach.

"I saw him in his office and we talked a little. This and that. His mind seemed to be on something else. When I got ready to go, he said, 'Alf, you ought to stick around tonight. I'm going to have something to say in the morning and you'll probably want to hear it.'

"I asked him if he could tell me now, so I could get going, and he said no, he couldn't. But he was sure I'd want to stick around to hear it. And that's when I knew what it was.

"I said, 'Coach, is this what I think it is?' He said yes, and then he just started crying. He cried like a baby. Just couldn't help himself. You get that way when you have a heart condition, like he did. I have one myself, so I know.

"Anyway, he got himself pulled together and he told me that he was going to be making the announcement in the morning, at a press conference. I told him I had to call the paper and tell them to get ready. This was just too big for us to do like an ordinary press conference. We'd need front page space. More reporters here. Stories on his whole career. He didn't want me to do it but I just told him, 'Coach, it's too big.' And finally I made the calls."

(Van Hoose was actually scooped on the story by Herschel Nissenson, who covers college football for the Associated Press. Nissenson had a tip from New York, where Perkins had told his Giants players that he was leaving. So Nissenson broke both Bryant's retirement and the name of his successor. He said it was his most satisfying accomplishment in journalism.)

The next morning, dry-eyed and gracious, Bryant announced that he was retiring as head football coach of the University of Alabama. He would remain as athletic director. Ray Perkins, currently head coach of the professional New York Giants, would replace him as head football coach. He said, predictably, that he'd "done a poor job of coaching," and that "the players deserve better."

There was one more game to play, the Liberty Bowl in Memphis. Bryant's first bowl team from Alabama had played in the first Liberty Bowl, so there was a nearly classical symmetry to Bryant's career. Alabama, of course, won the game. How could it not have?

Bryant said, many times, that he would "croak in a week," if he quit coaching. But friends thought maybe, at 69, he had changed his mind and decided to stick around and enjoy some living away from the football field. He talked about bird hunting trips he wanted to take. Golf he wanted to play. Time he wanted to spend with his grandchildren.

He was at Jimmy Hinton's house for dinner one night and had trouble breathing. He was taken to the hospital in Tuscaloosa, where the diagnosis was that he'd had a heart attack. He was in no danger, they said. But after the kind of attack he'd had, there was always the threat of another, usually much more severe, coming in the first twenty-four hours. If he made it through that danger period, the prognosis would be excellent.

He was sitting up in bed the next morning, making phone calls. He was trying to help one of his old assistants get a coaching job somewhere. And he was following through on a bond order he had placed the day before with Jerry Duncan, the tackle eligible from the old sixties team that won national championships.

Then, early in the afternoon, a massive heart attack killed

him. "It would take just one hell of a damned big one to stop *that* heart," one of his old friends said. Bear had lasted six weeks from the day he quit, instead of one. The doctors said his retirement had nothing to do with the heart attack and some people accepted that.

He was buried in Birmingham, sixty miles from Tuscaloosa. The cortege traveled the interstate between the cities and every overpass was crowded with people who had come to see Bryant come this way for the last time. There were hand-painted signs everywhere, one of which said, "God must have needed an offensive coordinator." Trucks and traffic pulled off the road as the funeral procession passed. One big trucker with "Roll Tide" stickers on his bumpers took off his baseball cap and wiped his eyes.

Old players, coaches who had opposed him, friends, and strangers came to Birmingham to bury Bryant. Lee Roy was there. Joe Namath. Darrell Royal. Woody Hayes. The *New York Times* and the networks sent people to cover the funeral.

More than half a million people attended the services or viewed the procession. The casket was covered in red and white carnations. The pallbearers were all members of his last team. Before the service, the organ played "Amazing Grace" and "A Mighty Fortress Is Our God." The words read over his body were "I will not leave you comfortless . . . peace I leave with you. My peace I give to you."

He had come a long way from Moro Bottom and, just as he would not be denied in life, he would not be forgotten in death. As Eddie Robinson, the Grambling coach who eventually broke Bryant's record—and who also attended the funeral in Birmingham, a black coach from an all-black school—said, "As long as they kick it off, there will be something of Coach Bryant in the game."

7

The Tie That Blinds

With ten days remaining until the Alabama/Auburn game, the *Crimson White*, Alabama's student newspaper, appears with a prominent ad calling for Ray Perkins's head. JERK THE PERK, the display type reads. When the fans go after a college coach, they first look for an alliterative campaign slogan. During the ordeal of Jerry Faust at Notre Dame, the war cry of the suffering fans was "Oust Faust." If Pat Dye ever wears out his welcome at Auburn the bumper stickers will probably say "Bye Bye to Pat Dye," or somesuch.

To a visitor unfamiliar in the ways of Alabama football, it seems odd for the paper to be running this ad on the eve of the Auburn game, after a win over Southern Mississippi and a season that stood 7–2–1. The losses were to Tennessee and Penn State, both by two points. Penn State was currently undefeated and ranked number one in the nation. Tennessee had lost once to Florida, and will win the conference if it can get by Kentucky and Vanderbilt. Spoiled by Bryant, Alabama fans expect to beat everyone and become restless, sullen, and rude when they don't.

114

Donnez moi une break, one New York sportswriter who has formed an attachment to Alabama football likes to say. It seems the appropriate response to the newspaper ad.

Actually, the visitor learns, the most recent particular in the list of charges against Perkins is neither of those losses, though they hurt. What has Alabama fans hot these days is the one tie on this year's record. There is something . . . well, *shameful* in that tie. Probably no other fans in the world would feel so strongly about a draw. It goes back, into the lore of Alabama football, to the time when Perkins himself played. But first, there is the matter of this year's tie, the one that has fans so agitated in 1985.

The tie came early in November, against Louisiana State, an old and fierce rival. They played in Baton Rouge, in a stadium that fans and the press like to call "the Tiger Pit." The stadium holds 80,000 and, at any game, most of them will be fanatical supporters of the LSU Tigers, the "Bayou Bengals." Louisianans love a good time, and a football game, anywhere in the South, is about as good a time as there is. So they come to roar. In the old days, they played here at night and the fans would come, full of Cajun passion and liquor, and they would fill that stadium with more noise than seemed humanly possible. It was as if all of Mardi Gras had been poured into the oval then spilled out over its sides. The LSU home field advantage was a very real thing.

The first half was all Alabama, in spite of the crowd noise. Early in the first quarter, the team drove more than 70 yards for a touchdown. But the LSU defense was tough, as always, and Alabama could not score again in the half on any of three good opportunities. The normally reliable field goal kicker, Van Tiffen, missed from 46 yards and at the half Alabama led 7–0.

The second half was LSU's game. In the third quarter, they scored two quick touchdowns and Alabama stalled, which it had been doing all year. It was 14–7 when the fourth quarter began. In the Bryant era, Alabama fans would have considered the game as good as won. His teams seemed always to win when they went into the fourth quarter a little bit behind. It was one of their trademarks, one of the things that made their supporters proudest of them.

But this year's team had lost two that were close going into the fourth quarter. It looked like they were about to lose another when Van Tiffen missed a second medium-range field goal. The LSU fans, sensing a victory over a hated rival, began to yell louder and louder until the stadium seemed to throb like an overpowered stereo speaker under the volume of the cheers.

The Alabama fans—and a number had come to town for the game—were quiet and, in some cases, mutinous. This was a game, they thought, that the team could have, and should have, won. The kind of game, they grumbled, that Bryant would have *for sure* won.

Then, with less than three minutes left, Alabama got the ball near its own thirty for what would probably be its last chance to score again. The team began moving. Hesitantly, at first, and then with more confidence. The Alabama quarterback, Mike Shula—son of Don Shula, the head coach of the professional Miami Dolphins—moved the team into LSU territory. On a third and eight, when he came up over the ball, he changed the play that had been signaled in by the coaches, ran a quarterback draw, and gained eleven yards for a first down. On that play, he looked cool enough to play for his father, just like Ray Perkins had.

But the drive stalled once more. It was suddenly fourth down, nineteen yards to go for a first down. Still thirty to the goal line, with slightly more than a minute left to play. Shula had pulled one out, like this, in the first game of the season, against Georgia. When he lined the team up to go for this one, the crowd was roaring. It was dark now and the stadium lights had come on. It was like the old days for LSU fans, when they played them all at night, and they had special teams with names like the Chinese Bandits.

There was a wild, nocturnal quality to the scene. Against

the darkness, the noise seemed to rise another order of volume.

Shula dropped back. Waited. Waited some more. In the stands, Alabama fans shouted, "Throw it, Mike, *throw it*," and the LSU fans screamed, "Get him, *get him*."

Shula threw to Al Bell, who had caught the pass that beat Georgia with less than a minute to go. Complete for twenty-nine yards. First and goal at the two. The noise rose to a new pitch.

On first down, Alabama scored on a trick play. Halfback Gene Jelks faked a run, then threw back to the quarterback, Shula, who made a good catch and was tackled hard in the end zone.

"They have to go for two," Frank Broyles of ABC told fans around the nation.

Of course they had to go for two. Alabama teams played to win. Nineteen years ago an Alabama team that Bryant described as the best he had ever coached went undefeated through eleven games. But that team was not ranked number one in the nation. Notre Dame was, after settling for a 10–10 tie against Michigan State, also undefeated, in a game that had been promoted as the duel of the century and turned out to be a conservative and dull affair. Ever since, Alabama fans had talked, with the heat of indignation, about that game between two big Yankee teams with their vast followings in the press, as though it were something dishonorable and a black mark on the game of football, which was meant to be played with nothing less than the reckless all-out passion for victory of . . . oh, Robert E. Lee.

So now, with everyone in the stands and those watching on television certain that Alabama would go for it and wondering if they had another trick play in their book, and, with the voice of ABC football, a former head coach himself (Arkansas), saying that they had no choice, Ray Perkins called a time out. Perkins, it should be remembered, was an All-American on the Alabama team in the year that Notre Dame played for the tie.

He talked to his assistants in the press box. Thought for

a few seconds and then he sent the Alabama kicking team into the field. Van Tiffen was straight. Instead of passing or running for two points, Alabama had settled for a tie.

When the Alabama team left the field, their fans were waiting in the tunnel to the locker room. One of them screamed to assistant coach Jimmy Fuller, "Hey you m——ker! You don't have any guts!"

Outside the dressing room, another fan yelled, over and over, in the direction of Perkins and kicker Tiffen, "In all my years of watching Alabama football, I have never seen anyone disgrace Alabama's name like you and Perkins."

Finally a trooper appeared. "Sir," he said to the fan, "if you don't leave this area, I'm going to help you leave."

The trooper persuaded him to leave, but nothing on earth or in heaven could change his mind about that other thing . . . that—hard, almost, to speak the word—that *tie*.

So, for the next week, all over the state, people had been talking about Perkins's decision to go for the tie. His explanation, to the press and to the people who called his Tuesday night radio show, was that he thought his defense might be able to get the ball back and put his team in a position to score, and win. But, he said, at the very least, "the players had played too well and fought too hard to leave the field as losers."

Sportswriters recalled other coaches who had played for ties. Some of the giants of Southern football had done it. Bobby Dodd of Georgia Tech and Johnny Vaught of Mississippi, to name two. It was even brought up that Bear Bryant himself had once kicked after a late touchdown against Tennessee, when a successful run or pass would have put Alabama ahead. But that was Bryant, and the football gods allowed his team to get the ball back on a Tennessee fumble, score once more, and win the game.

Napoleon, who once said that, above all else, a successful general must be lucky, would have loved Bryant. But he had been dead now nearly three years and Ray Perkins had replaced him. For which sin, among some fans, there could be no forgiveness.

Perkins, who had walked neck deep in controversy ever

since he took the job, dealt with his decision all week long. On his call-in show, he told one man his question was "stupid," and reminded another, "I'm the coach of this team and as long as I'm the coach, I'm going to make the decisions according to what I think is best for the team." Henry Ford, who once advised "Never complain, never explain," would have loved Ray Perkins.

After a closed practice, on the day the ad appears, Perkins says, simply, that he doesn't have time to think about things like that. He is thinking about Auburn. He does say that he doesn't think the fans who did the booing at Baton Rouge were "real Alabama fans. They might follow the team. Go to a game or two. And probably they bet a few bucks and, when they lose their money, they blame the team. The real Alabama fans support you when you really need it. Last year, when we were losing, I got a lot more letters and calls supporting me than chewing me out. And if I'd been a fan out there, last year, I might have written me a letter and got on my ass pretty good."

Regarding the fan in Baton Rouge, Perkins narrows his already intimidating eyes and says, "You know, it's a good thing *I* didn't hear him. I might still be in the jail over there."

He isn't kidding, either, the visitor thinks.

Later, the visitor talks to a man who is wise about many things, including football in the South. He has written about it for years and about many other things as well. He knew Bryant. He is a collector of Bryant stories. He loves Alabama and the South shamelessly and is not the least bit defensive about it. He says, "Of course it's flawed and irrational. That's what's so wonderful about it. I wouldn't want to live in a place that wasn't flawed and irrational."

This wise man prefers anonymity. He has written several books under pseudonyms, so to respect his wishes we will call him Rufus, since he sometimes writes in a style reminiscent of Agee.

"He's got two big problems," Rufus says, "first, he hasn't won enough football games. Of course, he's a hard worker and a smart coach and he might be able to do something about that if they give him enough time."

And the second problem?

Smile. Pause. A sad, country-wise shaking of the head. "The second problem is that he ain't Bear Bryant. And there's not enough time in all of eternity to change that.

"You see," Rufus goes on, "a lot of people who looked like Alabama fans were actually *Bryant* fans. And if Perkins had come in and won, right away, that would have diminished Bryant. It would have meant that anyone could come to Alabama and win. They hated him because he wasn't Bryant, and they wanted him to fail because he wasn't Bryant. He did everything they wanted him to do, you know. He did all sorts of things—fired the assistant coaches, including Donahue, changed sponsors on the TV show, changed the uniforms, got rid of the wishbone, changed the broadcasting team, and a lot more—to prove that he wasn't Bryant and didn't have his touch. And then he obliged them by having a losing season. I'm sure that he didn't intend it to be that way, but you could say he cauterized the wound. Burned the excess hate off. Now all that's behind him and, if he has a winning season, he'll be all right. No matter what happens from now on, he'll never be a threat to their idol.

"I'd say that right now he's third and long in his own territory, but if he wins against Auburn next Saturday, then he'll be out of the hole and driving. That's why the game is so important to him. Of course, it's important to Pat too. Nothing is worse than building up expectations and then disappointing people.

"The game is big for everyone in the state, of course. Always is. But it's especially big for the coaches. I don't know that there's ever been a more important Alabama/Auburn game . . . and that's saying something."

The Recruiting Wars

Late in the week, there is a slight lull. The fever seems to ease a little. People still talk football, but they talk other things too. Like the coaches always say, you have to watch out before a big game that you don't peak too early.

The visitor can still learn things about football and its grip on Alabamians. The place to look on Thursday will be the letters column of the sports section of the *Birmingham News*.

The letter writers today are concerned with ethics, correct football scholarship, and the fundamentals of loyalty. They are an accurate reflection of the things people are saying, all around the state.

The first, and longest, letter is concerned with the lessons implicit in Perkins's decision not to go for two in Baton Rouge.

Ray Perkins [writes Allan J. Chappelle of Birmingham] is not just a sports figure. Rather, he is a *teacher* at the University of Alabama. He is charged with the responsibility of educating young men laboring under him so that they might be exemplary citizens. What lesson did going for the tie teach those men?

I have marveled at their comments, as quoted in the newspapers, about how a "tie is better than a loss." . . . It is much more noble to have sought a high goal and fallen short than to have achieved numerous lesser goals that were all very easily attainable. (One wonders how attainable even the tie looked at fourth and twenty, but never mind.) I keep thinking of the story of the talents in the Bible and the fact that God reserved his very strongest condemnation for the servant who took the highest percentage route and simply buried his talent in the ground. . . .

The goal of winning the game was well within the Alabama players' grasp. They were given an opportunity to achieve something truly great with talent that was capable of accomplishing the task and yet that opportunity was taken away from them by their teacher who was more concerned about the effect of their losing. The effect of their tying that game could have a much more significant impact on the lives of all those men, in a negative fashion, than a loss could ever have had.

The next letter writer was willing to give up the high theological ground and go straight up to the greatest temporal authority of all. Ronnie McCarty of Quinton wrote:

In light of all the commotion over Alabama Coach Ray Perkins' decision to go for the tie against LSU, and with all the "experts" stating that they *know* what Coach Paul "Bear" Bryant would have done, I have a quote some may find interesting.

The quote is found on page 197 of the book *Building a Championship Football Team*, published by Prentice-Hall and written by the late Coach Bryant. Under the heading "Game Strategy for the Quarterback," item No. 3 states: "You are playing for a victory, but remember, a tie is better than a defeat."

On the matter of loyalty to the team, Andrew Holcolmb of Hackleburg writes:

> This "fair weather" fan (the one who had to be escorted from the Alabama dressing room after the LSU game) shouldn't even be allowed to enter the stadium. I think Perkins has done a terrific job with the Crimson Tide. The team has gone through many changes and adjusted very well.

Finally, Glenda Wakefield, of Warrior, had this to say regarding the matter of Bo Jackson's courage:

> I would like to say we are very proud of Bo Jackson. He has contributed so much to Auburn football. We understand that he is human and is subject to injury. Anyone who has knowledge of his record is aware of his contribution.
> We want him to know that the true Auburn fans are extremely proud of him. We love him and the Auburn team.

For the next week, right up until kickoff, all these matters will remain under discussion. But gradually one topic will take over most conversations. The game. But for now, fans are still talking about that tie in Baton Rouge and Bo's courage . . . or lack thereof. And, more and more, almost as if to take their minds off this season, as it reaches its climax, they are talking, indirectly, about seasons to come. That is . . . they are talking about recruiting.

As the weekend approaches, recruiting is an appropriate topic. High school teams are in the semifinal stage of the tournaments for statewide championships in each of the various divisions. The boys who are starring in these games will be making the big plays for either Alabama or Auburn next year and in the years after that. There may be one player Friday night who will do for one school or the other what Lee Roy Jordan or Pat Sullivan or Ken Stabler or Bo Jackson did for his school.

The people who follow college football passionately also

pay close attention to recruiting. At a closed dinner earlier this week, which was hosted by a group of Alabama alums called the "Red Elephant Club," an Alabama assistant coach was asked as many questions about recruiting as he was asked about the Auburn game. The men at the dinner knew the names of the best high school ballplayers in the state, "the blue chippers," and they wanted to know how Alabama stood with each of them.

Recruiting was once an activity that depended on word of mouth to transmit information. Now it is a big, national business and, consequently, there are services that rate high school football players and send out information on them to people willing to subscribe to newsletters and magazines. "It used to be that they told you about how big a kid was, how fast he was, and what school he was leaning toward," says Kirk McNair, who publishes magazines devoted to sports at both Alabama and Auburn. "Now, they've got all that and the kid's grade-point average. That's important too, with the new NCAA rules."

Recruiting never really stops, even in the week before the biggest game of the season. Ray Perkins and Pat Dye will each attend one of those semifinal games in the high school playoffs on Friday night. They will be there to watch a player, or players, they want to recruit. They are not allowed, by NCAA regulations, to talk to those players. This would constitute an "illegal contact," but the player will know that they were there and this information will, presumably, help influence him.

"The rules are crazy," says an Alabama assistant on Friday. He is explaining recruiting to the curious visitor as they eat lunch with three or four other men, at Dreamland, a rib shack outside of Tuscaloosa where they serve slabs of pork drenched in a red sauce that is sweet, sour, and smokey all at the same time.

"You are not allowed to talk to the recruit at his home or school until after December first. That's why Coach is going to see him tonight, in a game, but won't be talking to him after. The recruit can come to visit the campus as many times as he wants, on his own. That's called an

Bear Bryant and Shug Jordan at Shug's last game.
Birmingham News Photo

Bear Bryant watches his last game as Alabama coach.
Birmingham News Photo

Ray Perkins. The first thing you notice about him is the stare.
Barry Fikes for 'BAMA Magazine

Pat Dye. The first word anyone uses to describe him is "tough."
Johnny Lawrence

Bo Jackson piling up the yards.
Birmingham News Photo

Ray Perkins in conference with his quarterback Mike Shula.
Barry Fikes for 'BAMA Magazine

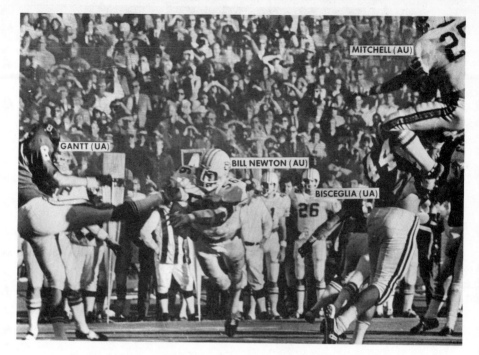

MITCHELL (AU)

GANTT (UA)

BILL NEWTON (AU)

BISCEGLIA (UA)

1972: "Punt 'Bama Punt." One of the two Auburn blocked that day.
Birmingham News Photo

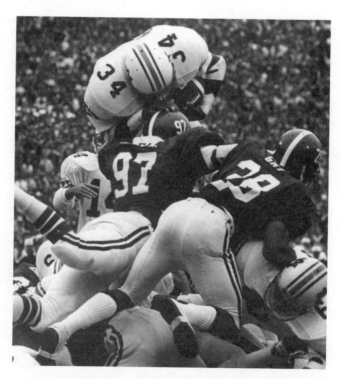

1985: Bo goes over the top to put Auburn ahead.
Birmingham News Photo

But Auburn drives again. *Barry Fikes for*
'BAMA Magazine

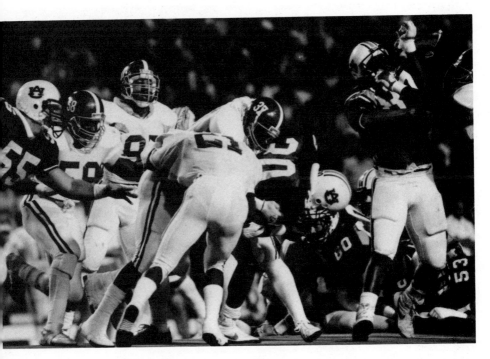

Then Gene Jelks breaks a long one for Alabama.
Barry Fikes for 'BAMA Magazine

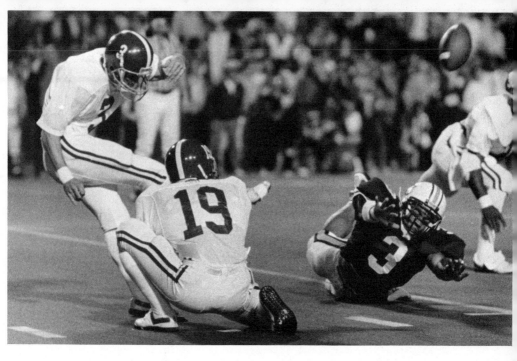

So it comes down to this kick . . .
Birmingham News

. . . by Van Tiffen. Alabama–25, Auburn–23.
Barry Fikes for 'BAMA Magazine

Tucker Frederickson caught the pass that beat Alabama and Joe Namath, 10–8. *Auburn University Photographic Services*

Pat Sullivan beat Alabama twice, and won the Heisman. *Auburn University Photographic Services*

(Upper left) "If they stay between the sidelines, Lee Roy will get
'em." Bear Bryant on Lee Roy Jordan.
University of Alabama Sports Information Office
(Upper right) "He can't run, he can't pass, and he can't kick—all
he can do is beat you." Bear Bryant on Pat Trammell.
University of Alabama Sports Information Office
(Above) Bear Bryant and Ray Perkins in other days.
Thomas R. Koeniges in Look Magazine

'unofficial visit.' We can pay for him to come once. That's an 'official visit.' He's allowed one of those to five different schools. Except for the official visit, you can't give a kid anything. And I mean *anything*. Not money for the picture show, not a T-shirt, not *anything*. The rule book is about that thick." His fingers show a space that is wider than the slab of ribs on his plate.

"The thing is, you've got all these rules and you've got people getting put on probation for rinky-dink violations and, at the same time, there are people being bought off for money. Very big money. And everybody knows it. Once in a while, someone will get caught. But most of them don't."

The college recruiting scandal is a perennial drama in American sports. The money grows larger and larger. The degree of outrage, on the other hand, seems to shrink. In the fall of 1985, when a Louisville newspaper reported recruiting violations in the University of Kentucky basketball program, the fans were furious—at the newspaper. The reporters on the story were threatened and some powerful members of the community muttered about an advertising boycott. Overall, cheating in college sports is considered normal. But the cheating must follow the accepted forms. It is permissible to buy recruits but not to bribe officials. The analogues are plentiful in American life. In politics, it is acceptable to give to a political action committee which then gives to a candidate. Direct gifts are unacceptable. Hell, man, those are *bribes*.

People with money are willing to spend it, virtually as much as it takes, to make sure the old school wins . . . or the loophole passes. The people in a position to make it happen—football players and politicians—are not generally born rich and are paid much less than they could make selling their services in the marketplace. A running back who stands six foot three, weighs two-thirty, and does the forty in 4.2 with the pads on could, in a free market, command a million, easily, for signing with just about any major football school.

A player is *allowed* room and board, books, tuition. Twenty years ago, he could get fifteen dollars a month laundry money, but that isn't permitted these days. So, not surprisingly, there is a flourishing underground economy in football players.

In football circles, everyone has a recruiting story. As he bites into another rib at Dreamland, the Alabama assistant tells the one that is going around at the moment.

"There's a kid everybody is after. One of the assistants from another school is sleeping with his mother."

"Kind of hard to top that," somebody else at the table says. "What do you do, send in *your* assistant who is the best at that?"

"The thing is . . . that's probably not an illegal recruiting technique. But if you gave the kid a ticket to the picture show one slow Sunday afternoon, that would be a violation."

Somebody tells the story of another player who was being chased by everyone. Came from a family with nothing, according to the story, and one day he just started driving around in a brand new BMW. "The really outrageous thing was that he had these personalized plates on the car. His own name on the license plates. Used to be a guy would kind of try to *hide* the car a little. Be discreet about it. This guy wanted everyone in town to know that he'd hit big with some school."

"That's the kind of thing," another one of the lunchers says, "that I don't understand. A suitcase full of hundred dollar bills is one thing. I mean, how is the NCAA going to track that down. Hard enough for the IRS. But a *car*, you'd think that would be easy."

"And cars aren't the worst. How about a house?"

"A *house*?" the visitor says. "A player will actually take a house?"

"Not the player. His parents. You see kids with their hands out, but a lot of the time what they're thinking is a stereo, you know. Or a motorcycle. It's the parents who tend to think big. They know more—or think they do—about how to play one school off against the other. And sometimes you'll see a family with a son who plays a great game of linebacker moving from a little tract house out to a big place on the hill with a view and some land and maybe even a pond. And Dad is still working for the power company.

"But then, you're just as likely to run into parents on the other side. People living in a little house, raising a big family, who'll say to you, 'I didn't bring 'em up to sell 'em. You say you'll give him room and board, tuition, and books. Now tell me, Coach, are you going to see to it that he studies? Because wherever my boy goes to college, I want to make sure he gets a good education.' Those are the ones you love.

"See, a coach who is a good recruiter, working for a good program, one that doesn't cheat, doesn't mind going back again and again to visit people like that. Everyone is a little bit of a salesman and if you're proud of the program, then you actually like selling it. Even though it means you're on the road a lot and away from your family. What you hate, when you're recruiting, is to see the alums come in. They are the loose cannons. Some schools can control them better than others and some don't even try."

"And," one of the other men says, "the alums can be pretty creative. I mean, it's not all satchels of money and brand new cars." Then he tells a story, as he sops up the remaining bar-b-que sauce with a slice of porous white bread.

The story is about a player from down in the southern part of the state. Everybody wanted him. "He was the kind of kid who could take you to the national championship. You could build a team around him. Everybody wanted this kid.

"Well, he didn't have his hand out, like some of them. And when you run into a situation like that, what a lot of alums do is try to find what it is the kid wants without even knowing he wants it. That way, you can do the kid a favor and he'll be grateful.

"Turned out this kid had an older brother who had dreams of becoming his own boss. He wanted to get into the pulp-wood business. He had enough to buy the chain saws and hard hats and to lease some cordage. But he was a long way from having the money he needed to buy a logging truck. And he'd never borrowed enough at the bank to even have a credit rating.

"The banker who heard this decided to go ahead and gamble on the fellow and give him a line of credit, since it sure would help the old school out if the little brother went there on scholarship.

"And that's how it all happened. Big brother got a line of credit so he could buy a pulpwood truck and little brother appreciated it so much that he went to school where the banker had gone to school. Won a lot of games for them, too. He's a starting professional quarterback now. And, you know, I'm not so sure that any of that stuff was illegal. And I'm certainly not sure, if it was illegal, that it *ought* to be illegal. It seems to me that the whole world pretty much does business that way and to say that football can't is unfair and stupid."

Everyone at the table agreed, more or less, with this assessment. The old boy network is standard business practice, they nodded. No question about it. But what about outright cash gifts? Those can't be sanctioned, can they?

"Nah. But you have to understand that they are hard to control, in the first place. A guy who likes to shake hands with athletes and leave them holding hundred dollar bills is going to be a hard man to reason with. Sometimes the athletic department really does not know what those guys are doing. And a lot of people think the players ought to get *something*, since they bring in millions to the university. Their time and pain ought to be worth something.

"And then, there is the matter of how you punish the people who break the rules. The way it is now, the whole school gets punished. No bowl games, no television games. You might lose some scholarships. That can happen even if it is only one alum, giving money to one or two players. The whole team gets put on probation. And you know what happens to the alum? Nothing. He's been bribing people, is what he's actually been doing, and nothing happens to him. He might even be a hero to some of the other alums when they find out how much he was giving, how hard he was trying.

"The player who was taking the bribes doesn't usually get punished in any specific way, either. He's on probation, like the rest of the guys on the team. But a lot of them are honest and he's crooked. Still, they are paying the same penalty."

So what, the visitor asks, can be done?

"Well, what I think ought to be done is you ought to find a way to hurt the guy who makes the bribes. But that would be real hard. And you ought to hurt the guy who takes the bribes without hurting the rest of the team. That's easy.

"Then, if you've got a coach who is working with alums to bribe players, or knows about alums who are doing it and keeps quiet, you kick him out of the college game. Make the people who are out there committing the actual crime pay the penalty instead of spreading it around the whole program.

"I'd make one more change, too. I'd pay the kids *something* above the table, so they could buy clothes and go out. You can't believe how poor some of these guys are. You go out to recruit him and you go to his house and you realize that he comes from a family that doesn't have two nickels to rub together. I mean old-fashioned, red dirt, country poor where you've got ten people living in three rooms and chickens scratching in the yard. I just think you ought to be able to pay them a little something. Some people say you're already paying them a lot when you give them a free education, but still. . . .

"And I'm the first to admit, even if the NCAA did everything exactly my way, you know what would happen?

"People would still cheat. There might be a little less of it. But there'd still be some. People would cheat because it's human nature and football brings out the best, and the worst, in human nature. That's probably why people like football so much."

There are coaches in football now who are reformers. They are loudly against payoffs and against the sort of football programs that keep players for five years then send them out into the world without a diploma or any particular skills except those directly related to football. There have always been coaches like this in the college game. Call them idealists. At one time there were quite a few of them among the ranks of the winners. But then, a newer breed came along and many of this breed were vaguely proud of their lack of idealism, projecting an attitude of "Come on, man, we are talking big time football, here. Don't give me a lot of this 'student athlete' crap. That went out with the single wing and one-platoon football."

These coaches won and they moved from school to school and they got bigger and bigger contracts. Jackie Sherrill, who played at Alabama with Ray Perkins, went from Pittsburgh, where he won a national championship, to Texas A&M for a salary of more than a quarter of a million a year. His contract included all sorts of insurance policies and country club memberships and ran for five years with automatic annual renewals, which meant that if he did get fired, buying out the contract would cost the A&M alums about a million and a half, which is a lot of money even if you are Texas rich. There was great controversy and a degree of dismay in the academic community over Sherrill's fat contract. Sherrill defended himself, saying "Football is a business, let's get our heads out of the sand." (Late in 1985 a recruiting scandal was brewing around Texas A&M. A newspaper series reported numerous cash payments and other "irregularities." Sherrill claimed to have investigated them and found himself, and his program, innocent.)

But just as this new breed of coach seemed to have triumphed, a newer and tougher breed of coach arrived in college football. The man who typifies this new style of coach is Bill Curry, Ray Perkins's old friend and his teammate on the Baltimore Colts.

Curry is head coach at Georgia Tech, where he once played. He came into that job when Tech was down and announced that he would bring the school back to glory without cheating.

In 1984 and 1985 Curry's team beat the rival University of Georgia, which was embarrassed after the season ended by a widely covered lawsuit in which a former Georgia faculty member claimed she was fired for not giving preferential treatment to athletes. The president of the University eventually resigned as a result of the trial and subsequent scandal. But Vince Dooley, the coach and athletic director, did not. As football people like to point out, at Georgia the athletic department was not on trial. The administration was.

The Georgia scandal is interesting and will no doubt be the subject of books and perhaps even a movie. But it probably raised more questions than it answered. There are deep, fundamental problems in college sports today. In all sports, for that matter. Trite to say, but there are good and bad aspects to college sports. Ray Perkins might still be working in a filling station if it had not been for football. Eighty thousand people are willing to sit in the stands at Georgia and watch young men, like Perkins, play football. As Dan Jenkins, author of *Semi-Tough*, says, they wouldn't pay to watch a math test. So football players are different, and it is naive to expect that they will not be treated differently. Harvard has a record of treating people according to shifting standards. Many of the Kennedys, for instance, might not have been admitted if their names had been different, their father had been poorer or, even, if their skin had been a different color. In the real world, the goal should be prudence, and what disturbs people like Bill Curry is that college football—and football in general—has gone beyond the prudential.

When Curry arrived at Tech, he came into a bad neighborhood. To the north of him, in South Carolina, there was Clemson, which had won a national championship in '82 but had also been put on probation. To the south, there was Florida, which had been poised to win a national championship in 1984 when scandal hit the school. It was put on probation and the coach, Charlie Pell (another former Bryant player), was fired in disgrace. To add to Curry's problems, Tech was a private engineering school with high academic standards which it would not relax for the sake of a winning football program.

Curry said, "One of the things that really troubled me, when I started out recruiting, was finding that the standards for athletes had been relaxed down into the high school. I was finding ballplayers who'd been straight-A students who'd never taken a course in algebra. That's horrible."

Curry said not only would Georgia Tech not compete by using illegal recruiting techniques, it would also turn in any school it knew to be guilty of breaking the rules. "Basics have to come to the front when you are responsible for a lot of kids who are seventeen to twenty-one years old. You've got to set an example or ten or fifteen years down the line they'll be cheating and the IRS will be coming after them for it and you'll be partly responsible."

Other coaches had talked that way. But most of the idealists lost. Especially at schools with academic requirements as tough as those at Tech. But Curry won. He won his conference two years in a row and he has Georgia Tech back on top. As the NCAA gets tougher on recruiting violations and stricter on academic standards, he may become more and more the model football coach. "You see more and more of us. Perkins, Ken Hatfield, Bobby Ross up at Maryland. Steve Sloan. It seems like there is less cheating now than when I came into college coaching, in '82," Curry says. "There is less of it, and it is less blatant. But it is still there."

Alabama and Auburn have both recruited successfully over the years. That's obvious. But Alabama has never been on probation, while Auburn has achieved that unhappy distinction three times in the last twenty-five years. This included 1957, when they were undefeated and national champions but could not go to a bowl game because they were on NCAA probation.

Alabama, so far as anyone knows, has never even been

investigated by the NCAA. In the Southeastern Conference, only Vanderbilt and Tennessee, other than Alabama, could make that claim before this year. And after this football season, a scandal would hit Tennessee, much to the satisfaction of many other schools in the conference, since the Tennessee coaches and athletic director were known for their piety and holier-than-thou attitude. It was they who insisted that Florida be stripped of its conference championship in 1984, after the NCAA had found it guilty of recruiting violations. "Couldn't happen to a nicer bunch of guys," a member of the Auburn Athletic Department said when he heard about Tennessee's troubles.

Once he started winning at Alabama, Bryant could bring players there because they wanted to play for him and win. Auburn had a much tougher time of it inside the state, but that changed when Bryant was near the end of his career. More and more boys would wonder aloud if Bryant would be there for the whole four years and he would say, "Son, I can't promise you I'll be at Alabama as long as you will."

Other coaches took advantage of this. Especially Pat Dye, who knew how it was done because he'd done it for Bryant. He beat his old boss recruiting inside the state for at least two years running.

One of the boys Bryant lost to Auburn was Ben Tamburello, who is an All-American center and a candidate for the Outland Trophy, which goes to the best lineman in college football. Tamburello remembers going to Tuscaloosa for a visit after he had told Ken Donahue he would be going there, on scholarship, the next year. But this was a weekend when Alabama had lost, in Tuscaloosa, to Southern Mississippi. It was not a happy time, and at the athletic dormitory Bryant barely spoke to Tamburello or his parents.

"He just mumbled something to us in the dining room. He didn't seem to care much about us. He seemed real tired."

Dye had not given up on Tamburello and after that weekend, in Tuscaloosa, Auburn looked better and better.

Finally, Tamburello changed his mind. He called Bryant to explain.

"He listened and then he said something that I still don't understand," Tamburello says. "He told me if I was the kind of person that would change his mind like that then maybe I belonged at Auburn."

A little later, Bryant decided he'd had enough. "He probably would have liked to go another season. But he saw there were big problems ahead and knew the longer he stayed, the worse they would get."

So now the recruiting wars are fought by Perkins and Dye. Perkins won, by all accounts, last year. The win against Auburn at the end of the year helped. It gave his program a lift. Also, ironically, the fact that Dye had done so well began to work against him. A team that is very deep in talent sometimes looks too formidable to a recruit and he quickly goes where he thinks he can play, and contribute, instead of sitting on the bench. Perkins was playing a lot of freshmen at Alabama because he had to.

But that was last year. This is another year. Alabama has had a better season than anyone expected. Auburn has not done as well as people believed it would. But the teams have almost identical records. So the winner of the game will be the team that goes into the last quarter of the recruiting season with—the word is inevitable—momentum on its side.

"There's a lot more at stake here than a game," the assistant coach says to the visitor, prying Dreamland pork gristle from his molars with a toothpick. "Selling is a whole lot easier when your product is a winner."

Still in the Hunt

Football is not the whole point of life in Alabama during November. There is also hunting. But at the hunting camps these days there is always a television so the hunters can keep up with football. And when they aren't out in the woods, the hunters are sitting around camp talking about football. You can't escape that anywhere in Alabama in November.

The deer season opens and on the Saturday before the Alabama/Auburn game, the clubs around the state put on their first drives of the year. A lot of men look forward to this day the same way they look forward to the game. It is a time that makes the rest of the year worth surviving.

There are some, of course, who haven't survived and, at Dollarhide, the most famous hunting camp in the state, the members (Alabama people, all of them) will miss Riggs Stephenson. They buried him one week before the first hunt. He was eighty-six and one of the great names in Alabama football. He was an All-Southern back in 1920 and then went on to play major league baseball for fourteen years. He retired with a lifetime batting average of

143

.336, which Alabama sportswriters thought qualified him for the Hall of Fame. He was never selected and his old friends are still bitter about the slight.

But as they arrive at Dollarhide, in Greene County, on the banks of the Warrior River on Friday afternoon, the members don't talk about the Hall of Fame. Occasionally, when one member greets another, he will say, "Beautiful day. Just beautiful. I believe we're going to have a fine hunt. Shame Riggs won't be here to see it."

"Surely is," the other member will say. "It surely is."

They begin arriving sometime in the early afternoon at the clubhouse, which sits at the end of a long, raggedly blacktopped road that runs through bean and cotton fields, past the small unpainted and undistinguished homes of the black families that now own, and farm, most of this land. There are young men who will be playing in the big game, one week from now, who grew up in homes like these, a visitor thinks as he drives by.

The clubhouse is a suitably ramshackle affair, with several outbuildings for tools and tractors standing around a lawn that is shaded by old pecan and oak trees. There is something quiet and ageless about these trees and some of the same feeling extends to the clubhouse, which looks, with its screen doors and its old, rough wooden sides, like it has been here forever, or at least since the end of the Civil War, when Union cavalry rode through and burned everything, just as they burned the University of Alabama, some sixty miles north.

There is a large screen porch behind the cabin. Several chairs, old and unpainted, sit on the porch along with a soft drink machine that has been altered to accommodate canned beer and a large metal icemaker. Two men sit on the porch in the old chairs under mounted sets of deer antlers bleached white with age. They are having a drink and watching as the cars arrive on the lawn and the passengers get out. They call names as they recognize faces.

"Hello, Tandy."

"Hello, Wu."

"Seen Joe?"

"He's in there somewhere."

"Got somebody for him to meet."

"Hello, Tandy."

"Well, hello, Grafton."

The visitor is introduced to Grafton Hocutt, a lean man with lively, almost merry eyes, who seems to be in his seventies. Hocutt, it turns out, owns the largest funeral home in Tuscaloosa. He offers the visitor a drink and when he has it, takes him around the camp grounds. He shows him the meat pole, where the deer are hung when they are first brought into camp, and then the butchering shed. Hocutt, not surprisingly, supervises this part of the camp's operations.

At some point, the conversation turns to the topic of football—it always does—and the name Bryant comes up, inevitably, a few minutes later.

"Did you see that game, I believe it was the Cotton Bowl, on national TV where Roger Staubach asked him if he thought about Stagg and the record?"

No, the visitor says. He doesn't think he remembers that one.

"Well, it was after the game and he was being interviewed. When they asked him about it . . . the record, you know . . . he said that he wasn't worried about Pop Warner or Amos Alonzo Stagg. That there was only one man in the world he was worried about and that was Grafton Hocutt . . . his undertaker."

Hocutt smiles happily and the visitor laughs with him.

"When he died, you know, they wouldn't move him until I got up there, to the hospital, to make sure it was done right."

Hocutt continues the tour. The afternoon is cooling a little, and the light is showing the first shades of pink, when he finds Wu Winslett and introduces the visitor.

"Wu was the first AP All-American to play for Alabama," Hocutt says, beaming. "Get him to tell the story about the time he was on the train, coming back from Canada."

"Oh, the hell," Winslett says. He has a deep, impatient, growling sort of voice and a stern face with vast, brushy

eyebrows and vaguely Oriental features—the explanation
for his nickname. His teammates called him "Chink" until
a stage play called *Mr. Wu* came to Tuscaloosa and, from
that day, the name stuck. His real name is Hoyt.

Wu Winslett is the president of Dollarhide and eager to
take the visitor around for a look.

"Get in the jeep," he says gruffly, "and I'll take you for
the fifty-cent tour."

They drive down a firm, well-drained road cut through
the woods. The club owns nearly six thousand acres—some
ten square miles—of this bottom land. A lumber company
cruised it several years back, Winslett says, and offered
three million dollars to lease the timber rights. The club
members weren't interested.

It is easy, if you love the woods, to see why. Winslett
guns the jeep down the road. Closer to the river, the trees
rise more and more formidably on either flank. There is
oak big enough to make ship timbers, trees that are tall,
straight, and probably two centuries old, at least. There
are some fine-looking red gum and shag bark hickory. Also
a few tall pines, though this river bottom forest is largely
hardwood.

Winslett tells the visitor about the formation of the club,
which has been in some kind of existence since the late
nineteenth century. "The land was leased up until 1942.
Then we formed a new club, with forty members, and
bought it outright. The membership cost $250 plus another
$900 or so to pay off a note. Memberships can be passed
on, from father to son. Or they can be sold. The last one
to change hands went for $60,000, as part of an estate."

To make sure that owning a share, by inheritance, does
not bring any undesirables, there are two kinds of memberships, so it is theoretically possible to own stock—a
piece of the property—and still not be allowed on the hunts.
There are standing offers of $80,000 for memberships, but
no one is selling even though many members, like Winslett,
are in their seventies and eighties.

"Lot of people would like to be in Dollarhide. There

aren't many clubs that own anything this fine." Winslett takes one hand off the wheel and gestures toward the great woods, which have, if anything, grown even taller and more formidable this much closer to the river. The trees are so tall and have spread such a thick canopy that there is very little underbrush. You can see for half a mile or so, across clean ground, through the straight, thick trunks of the great oaks. It is restful and shaded among these trees. And quiet, when Winslett pulls off the road and turns the motor off. Being there, in this vast quiet . . . is like being in church.

Winslett drives to the point above a sweeping oxbow in the river. It is brown with mud, wide as a football field, and strong. "Some fish in there," Winslett says, "but we've got better fishing in our ponds."

He drops the jeep back into gear and takes the visitor back toward camp, showing him the ponds where members catch bass and shoot mallards.

"We've got just a hell of a problem with beaver," he says, as they pass a slough that spreads out behind a dammed-up creek.

Three tawny doe are feeding in a clearing and when the jeep comes around the bend, they turn and run into the woods. Their tails show brilliant, cottony white in the gloom.

The visitor asks Winslett about his football playing days.

"Went to two Rose Bowls—1925 and '26. In the first one, we beat Washington 20–19. We had just a hell of a team. Johnny Mack Brown. Pooley Hubert."

Winslett talks briefly about the trips across the country by train. "Pretty exciting for a country boy from Frenchman's Bend, never been anywhere before. We stopped to see the Grand Canyon. Took tours of the Hollywood studios when we got to Los Angeles." The visitor remembers pictures of Marion Davies presiding over the opening ceremonies of the 1925 game.

Those first two Rose Bowl games established Alabama and, by extension, southern football. But the struggle for recognition, even respectability, went on. (It still does, it sometimes seems, because the people in the South who

live and die football can't do without it.) A few years after
Winslett graduated, when another Alabama team went
west to play in the Rose Bowl, the governor of the state
put the feelings of many Alabama people—many Southerners—into bitter words.

"We have been hampered industrially," the governor
said, "by an unfair picture the world seems to have of
Alabama as a state of undersized, weak people living in
swamplands full of malaria and tuberculosis. None who
have seen [Coach Wallace] Wade's Tide in action, or who
read the account of the game for the next day, will continue
to embrace this idea."

The Alabama players who went west were smaller than
the athletes they went out there to play. But they were fast
and disciplined, and as underdogs they seemed to play
better. All of which satisfies the Southerner's sense of himself.

"Stanford had the best football players I've ever seen.
Big strong boys," Winslett says nearly sixty years later.
"And their coach was Pop Warner. He was one game be-
hind Stagg. Bryant passed them both."

Winslett says he knew Bryant a little. "Sold him an
insurance policy when he graduated Alabama. He wrote
to thank me when he was at Texas A&M and the policy
had matured. That fellow never missed a trick. He came
to Dollarhide once or twice. He'd play a little in the poker
game. But not much. It was too tame for him. He was a
Vegas man."

The sun has set when Winslett and the visitor return to
the camp house. More members and their sons and guests
have arrived by now. The sons, some of them men in their
forties, do the cooking. The kitchen is busy. The older men
relax, visit, enjoy a drink in front of one of the several
fireplaces.

"Did he tell you he was an All-American?" one of the
members asks the visitor when he sees him returning with
Winslett.

"Now come on," Winslett says.

"Tell him about the train, Wu. In Canada."

"You tell him," Winslett growls. This is evidently an old, old routine. One of the many Dollarhide rituals.

"Well," the member says happily, "Wu here was traveling. Up in Canada, a few years back. On the train with his wife. The train was in Canada but getting ready to cross the border and come back into the U.S. So the conductor is walking the aisles and saying 'All Americans. All Americans.'

"Wu jumped out of his seat and hollered, 'Right here. First team AP. End. 1926.' "

The visitor smiles. Winslett groans, and the other members all laugh, as they must have several hundred times now at this story.

"Let me introduce you to Joe," Winslett growls to the visitor. "You'll just get in trouble if you stay here with this bunch."

Joe, or "Mister Joe," to the younger guests, who all seem to make a point of speaking to him, is Joe Sewell, who *is* a member of baseball's Hall of Fame. He welcomes the visitor, who says that he is honored. Sewell is in his eighties and not as fit as Winslett, but his mind is sound and he doesn't mind talking baseball.

The visitor listens to his stories about Babe Ruth and Lou Gehrig. He and Gehrig roomed together, on the road, when Sewell was finishing his career with the Yankees. He tells about how he saw Ruth hit the famous called shot. "People say it didn't really happen. That it was just a story. But I know it happened because I *saw* it. I'd just flied out to Hack Wilson, hard, and I was sitting up on the steps of the dugout, watching, when Babe went up to the plate."

The visitor nods appreciatively. Sewell tells another story about Ruth arriving at the park dead drunk and going four for four. "When he first got to the locker room, he put his pants on backwards. I had to help him get dressed. He was just a big lovable baby," Sewell says. "An overgrown kid who just liked to have fun. Nobody even got mad at him when he did something like that."

He tells the visitor about hitting against Walter Johnson and Grover Alexander. His conversation is like a roll call of baseball immortals, and it plainly gives him as much pleasure to tell these stories as it does the visitor to listen to them.

This man, the visitor thinks, hit .312 lifetime and .352 in 1923. He was a tough hitter, probably the toughest ever to strike out. Only four times in two different seasons— something no one else has accomplished, even once. Barely one hundred times in his career of over 7,000 times at bat.

While he is talking to the visitor a young man comes up to Sewell and says, "Hello, Mister Joe, good to see you. I want you to know how sorry I was to hear about Mister Riggs."

"Thank you," Joe Sewell says.

The young man then says hello to several of the members who are sitting in large stuffed chairs in the back of the room. He says that he's sorry to be late, but that he ran into some trouble getting out of town.

"I was just going by the store, you see, to pick up a few things. I'd found a place in the lot and I was locking up when this car that was all orange and blue pulled up next to me. Had Auburn stickers all over it. 'War Eagle' painted on the windshield. The guy had on an orange hat, blue shirt and pants, and orange shoes. He starts yelling some-thing at me and then he pulls out a razor.

"And you know," the man says, deadpan, "I believe if he'd a had a place to plug it in he'd have killed me."

Everyone in the room groans.

Supper is chicken and greens and biscuits. When it is done the poker game starts in a room with a fireplace big enough to cook in, which is what it was built for back before the power line came down this far. Above the mantel there is a mounted set of antlers, locked up the way they were when some hunters came on two big bucks that had fought until their antlers tangled and then fell and died together. Next to the tangled antlers, there is a framed roster of the Alabama Sports Hall of Fame, with pictures of all the members. Wu Winslett's picture is there, along with Joe Sewell's. There are also pictures of Satchel Paige, Don

Hutson, Bear Bryant (of course), Johnny Mack Brown, Jesse Owens, John Heisman, Early Wynn, Shug Jordan, Riggs Stephenson, and others, white and black.

The big oak logs blaze and the drinks are poured and the cards are dealt and the lies and the jokes are told, and not a single man in the room who promised himself he was going to get to bed early so as to be clearheaded for the hunt has been able to keep his word. And probably no one ever expected to.

But, toward midnight, the poker players drop out, one by one. The remaining four or five decide to deal down. The fire burns down to a mound of hot, fist-sized coals.

One more beer, says one man to two others, sitting with him in front of the huge stone fireplace.

Sure, they say, can't hurt.

So he goes for more beer and when he comes back and when the tops have been popped, the three men begin one of those aimless conversations about football.

"What's the best game you have ever seen?"

"Oh, that's easy, never be another one like the one against Tech, where we won 16–15."

"Maybe that would be the one if you only counted games we won. That Notre Dame Sugar Bowl was a mighty good game."

"God, I wish you hadn't reminded me. It *still* hurts to think about that one."

"Yeah, man, ain't that the truth."

From games, the talk meanders, predictably, to players.

"This Shula, he could be a good one. Might even be another Trammell."

"Nah."

"You don't think so?"

"Nope."

"Well, why not?"

"Because there ain't *never* going to be another Trammell, that's why."

"Well . . . you might have something there. But you know, if I had to pick one quarterback, from all of 'em, it would be Snake."

"Yeah . . . Stabler. He was a piece of work, wasn't he."

"Did things his way."

"Everybody remembers how Bryant kicked him off the team, same way he did Namath. But what they don't know was that Joe was just drinking in a honky-tonk. It wasn't a jailing offense. Stabler, now, he was leaving school every day after practice and driving to Mobile in a Corvette to see some old girl. Stayed all night and drove back the next day, speeding all the way, to make it in time for practice."

"Wonder he didn't get killed."

"Another beer?"

"I got to make biscuits at four in the morning."

"Then you might as well have another beer. It's too late for you to feel any way but bad in the morning."

"Let's have another beer, then."

Through three or four more rounds they talk on about Coach Hank Crisp, who was "tougher than Bryant," remembering the way Crisp would wrap the stump of the arm he'd lost in a cotton gin in leather padding and use it like a club in scrimmages. Crisp had been there when Bryant was a player and he was still there when he returned as head coach.

Bryant wouldn't sign the contract until he knew there was a job somewhere for Coach Hank . . . somewhere that *wasn't* his staff.

Talk about Lee Roy because there is never a football conversation that doesn't include him.

"Made twenty-four tackles in the Orange Bowl game."

"I thought it was thirty-one."

"Probably was."

Talk, of course, about Bryant and how sick and weary he was at the end.

"No question but he knew he was going to die."

"Nope."

Talk about the game coming up.
  "This is the test for Perkins."
  "It's a long row to hoe."
  "I believe he can do it."
  "Dye is tough. You remember where he learned."
  "Same place Perkins did."
  "Matter of who learned best, then."
  "That's right. Now, what about one more beer?"
  "Might as well. But Lord, I hate to think about them biscuits."
  "Then don't think about them. Think about getting us another beer."

Breakfast comes at six, before the sun is fully up. There is coffee, first, to scald away hangovers. Eggs, grits, bacon, and biscuits with butter and molasses—as much to eat as you wanted—so a man won't have to be hungry in the woods.

After breakfast, with the morning still cool and just turning from gray to orange, about a hundred men, dressed in all manner of camouflage, hunter orange, khakis, and denim overalls—looking like the raggedest army the South ever put in the field—gather around Mr. Joe Sewell, who is master of the hunt at Dollarhide, to listen to instructions.

He wants everyone to be careful. To stay on their stands and not be moving around in the woods. The only people to be moving around in the woods are the drivers. Don't shoot any turkeys or any does. Don't shoot anything but buck deer, with at least four-inch spikes. Don't load your gun until you are on your stand and, when you leave your stand at the end of the hunt, make sure you unload your gun. Be sure of what you're shooting at. The dogs will be turned loose at eight o'clock and the hunt will end at eleven. Any questions?

There are no questions. The men all look at Mr. Joe. Vapor rises from their faces as they breathe easily and listen. Beyond the small circle of hunters, there are drivers—the men who follow the dogs through the woods—standing next to their pickup trucks, with their dogs held back, by leashes or in boxes, moaning in truck beds, eager to get on with the hunt. Now and then a dog will growl or bark, but no one pays any attention.

When Mr. Joe finishes, Wu Winslett steps up to remind the hunters that, "If anyone misses, he's going to have to answer to me."

"That's it, then," Joe Sewell says. "Let's have a good, safe hunt."

One of the men who stayed up late the night before, watches the departure of the hunters and says, "Now that's done, and I'm finished with those biscuits, I'm going back to bed. I've seen a deer before."

In thirty minutes, the hunters are all on their stands. (A "stand," in this case, is nothing more than a spot in the woods where a deer might be expected to come by, within gun range.) The noise of the last vehicle has died and the woods are once again quiet. Early morning birds sing a few notes and the squirrels stir the dry leaves in a search for acorns. Otherwise the morning is still. Almost hushed.

Then, at eight o'clock, the dogs are turned loose, and within a few minutes it is plain that one of them has struck a scent. His bark changes from something shallow and perfunctory that begins in his mouth to something much more urgent and deeper, that comes from the throat and beyond, down into his chest. It is a wild, primitive sound and it carries clearly through the woods and makes the hairs stand on the back of every waiting hunter.

Soon the woods are filled with the sound of dogs, and hunters look through the trees, in the direction where the howls sound closest, and wrap their hands around the stocks of their shotguns.

Someone fires. Three times. From a stand close to the river. The first shots of the morning. For a moment, the woods are quiet. And then the sound of the dogs, from several different locations, rises again.

The visitor has taken a stand perhaps a half mile from the river and is waiting under a towering white oak, listening to the sound of the dogs, which seems to pass from his ear directly into the blood. Most of the dogs are the usual hound breeds. Blue ticks, walkers, redbones, and plotts. There are also beagles and some bassets and a few mongrels that have some quality that makes them run deer.

This is the way that men have always hunted the bottom land in the South. They were doing it this way before the Civil War. It was the only way to hunt the bottoms then. The woods were so deep and weapons so primitive, that unless the dogs went in and chased the deer and got them moving, the hunters would never see game. Today, hunts like these still exist because . . . well, because this is the way that it used to be done and as long as there are still a few places around, like Dollarhide, with enough bottom land to hunt this way, people will keep on doing it. They like to hang on to things here.

The visitor is thinking about all this, his mind wandering across the connections between this and everything else around here, including football, with the howling of the dogs making a kind of fierce background music . . . when he hears the sound of something running across the carpet of dried leaves. As he listens, the noise grows louder and he knows that whatever is making the sound . . . is coming right for him.

He rises to one knee, grips his borrowed shotgun and strains to see through the lattice of thick tree trunks.

Four doe in a file come toward him, darting through the tree trunks as though through a maze or an obstacle course. Their tongues are outside of their mouths and their eyes are wide and wild. They are running in panic from the dogs. They never see the visitor who watches them run by, less than twenty yards away, before they are gone, blending into the background of trees.

This sector of the woods falls quiet. The visitor, full of biscuits and bacon and short of sleep, sits on the ground after carefully checking for snakes—there is a picture in the clubhouse of a six-foot diamondback killed by a visiting preacher. There are no snakes, and the visitor falls quickly asleep.

But not deeply asleep. He hears the sound of the dogs

and the occasional shot ringing out across the swamp. He imagines that he is listening, too, for the sound of another deer moving desperately across the dry leaves.

An hour passes. Two. The woods have warmed and the day will be hot. The visitor hears dogs . . . close and making game. He opens his eyes. Blinks back at the brightness. Then listens for the other sound. In a few minutes, he hears it.

He is on one knee when the deer comes in sight. A buck. Not a big one, but big enough by Mr. Joe's rules. Probably six points. This deer is moving more cautiously than the panic-stricken doe had. He knows the dogs are still a safe distance behind him and that it pays to watch ahead.

He comes in range. Stops. Looks in the direction of the visitor, who cannot shoot. He is a guest here, after all. A guest from the North. The gun he carries is more a prop than anything else. These are not his deer to shoot. So, he waves and the deer bolts. In a few minutes, there are shots from the next line of stands. The dogs come by a little later. Howling.

It is quiet for a minute and then there is an otherworldly sound. A yelp that the visitor knows comes from a man . . . but a man trying to sound like something else. *Whooooo uuuuup. Hoooowaaaahhh. Whoooooup. Hawwww.*

The man comes into view. He is a driver. Those were his dogs, running the little buck. He makes the sound so the dogs and, more important, the hunters will know where he is. Nobody knows why he makes *that* sound, anymore than anyone can say what an actual rebel yell sounded like. It sounded wild, is all anyone can say. So does this.

The driver stops making the sound when he sees the visitor.

"Why didn't you shoot?" he says. "Out of range?"

"Yes," the visitor says, grateful for the out. "But I think someone up ahead got him."

"Yeah. I got a look at him earlier. Little deer."

"Looked like it."

"But we jumped a big damned deer earlier. Old blue-backed swamp buck. Sounded like a truck roaring through the woods. Went straight for the river with four of my dogs on his trail. Swam the river and so did my dogs."

"Still over there?"

"I expect so. I'll be the rest of the weekend rounding them up, too. But that was sure a big buck. I'd like to have gotten a shot at him."

"I wouldn't have minded a look," the visitor says.

"They're still around . . . those big boys. A few of them. Not like it was, though."

The driver goes on after his remaining dogs, howling those strange notes as he walks off into the trees. In another half hour, the hunt is over and the trucks come down the logging roads to pick up the standers and take them back to the clubhouse. "How did you do?" someone asks the visitor.

"Fine."

"You get one?"

"No. But it was a great morning."

Back at the camp, the men stand clustered around the yard, drinking beer or sodas and talking about deer seen and shot, deer missed. A couple of members who skipped the drive to go fishing come into camp with a stringer full of nice bass.

"Now there's some boys with the right idea," one man says. "I could have been catching fish, instead of sitting out there looking for deer until my eyes hurt."

Five deer are brought in and hung on the meat pole. The one the visitor saw is among them. A young boy, out with his father, shot this deer.

One of the deer is a button buck. A male too young to have antlers. There are small knobs next to his ears where he would have had antlers, next year.

"Oh boy," someone says. "Mr. Joe ain't going to like that."

"Neither is Wu."

"Who shot him?"

"Some fellow from Georgia. A guest. He *says* he was shooting at another one, with antlers, and this one fell."

"Uh huh."

"I want to see him tell that to Wu."

"Yes, sir. That ought to be interesting."

Grafton Hocutt had placed a number ten can under one of the deer to collect the blood that runs down his neck and nose and drips to the ground. When all the hunters have returned, and the can is almost full, everyone gathers, as though signaled, around the meat pole. Wu Winslett steps up next to the hanging deer.

"All right. We're here to hand out punishments," he says. "Anybody here shoot and miss? Let's hear about it."

A boy, perhaps fifteen years old, steps forward. "Right here."

"Then come on up here and tell us how it happened."

"Well, sir, I was sitting with my back to him. I heard him out there and I turned just as slow as I could, but by the time I got turned around, he'd seen me and he was moving. I shot but I guess I missed him."

"You *guess*," Winslett says, his voice full of disapproval. "How many times did you shoot at him, boy?"

"Five."

"*Five*," Winslett says, almost shouting. "Well, bend over and take your punishment."

The boy bends over and Winslett gives him a lick with a smooth wooden paddle.

"Ah, hell," someone shouts. "You hit me a lot harder than that, Wu. You must be getting old."

"Who said that? Step up here and let's see if I'm getting old."

There is much hooting and laughter, but no one steps forward.

"All right. Anybody else here shoot and miss? I heard a lot of firing out there in the woods today and I don't see much hanging here in the way of results. So come on up here and take your punishment if you shot and missed."

Nobody comes forward.

"Well, I've never seen such a bunch of liars in my life."

"How about the man who shot that doe, Wu?" someone shouts.

"Don't worry, we're coming to that."

"All right," Winslett says, "we got some new boys, killed their first deer at Dollarhide today. Let's get one of them up here."

A young boy, perhaps fourteen, steps up. He has taken his shirt off and there are oval pads of muscle around his shoulders and chest, probably from weightlifting.

"All right, son," Winslett says, "tell us about it."

The boy describes how he shot his deer. What range, how fast the deer was moving, how many shots he took. He is proud and his voice shows it.

"Uh huh," Winslett says. "Well you look like you might be in pretty good shape. You play any football?"

"Yes, sir."

"You talk like you're pretty smart. Maybe even smart enough to play quarterback. That right?"

"No, sir."

"What *do* you play, boy?"

"Guard. Little linebacker."

"Uh huh. You ever meet an All-American?"

"Yes, sir."

"Who was it?"

"Steadman Shealy." (Shealy quarterbacked the last Alabama team to win the national championship, in 1979.)

The assembled men groan and laugh and whoop like the men driving dogs earlier that morning.

Winslett makes an elaborate face. "No," he says, "on second thought, you ain't smart enough to play quarterback."

"Show him how a real All-American does things, Wu," one of the men in the crowd shouts.

"Don't get it in his pretty *hair* now, Wu. Don't do *that*."

Winslett picks up the tin can full of deer blood and sticks his fingers in the thickening gore. He smears it on the boy's face, across his chest, and through his hair. The boy laughs and the men crowded around the meat pole shout and whistle.

"Give it to him Wu."

"*Now* ask him if he's ever met an All-American."

"All right, boy," Wu says tenderly, "that's enough for you. Go get cleaned up, now."

Two more young boys step up to get bloodied, including the one who shot the small buck that came by the visitor's stand. Winslett draws out their agony and the crowd enjoys the show. Through it all, there is increasing agitation for the man who shot the button buck.

"We're saving him for last," Winslett says. "Don't rush me."

Finally, it is the unfortunate's turn. He steps up next to the meat pole, stripped to the waist and wearing a look of pained, almost mortified embarrassment. Better to have missed . . . better not to have seen a deer . . . better to have stayed home.

"All right," Winslett says, "step up and show us your deer."

"It's the one on the end," the man says sheepishly.

"Go over and point to it."

The man does what he is told.

Winslett makes a face.

"Where are you *from?*" he says.

"Georgia," the man answers.

"*Georgia?* Is that what you call a buck in Georgia?"

"No, sir."

"You leave your glasses in Georgia?"

"No, sir."

"Well that deer's horns aren't even out of his hair yet."

"Yes, sir."

"All right. Step up here . . ."

After the ceremony by the meat pole, there is a big hot lunch. Greens and biscuits and meatloaf. Grafton Hocutt has finished his butchering and gives wrapped cuts of venison to the hunters who want some. There is a television in a back room of the camp house and the men gather around it eagerly to watch Tennessee play Kentucky. A Tennessee loss will keep alive Alabama's meager chance of a Sugar Bowl bid. But Tennessee is strong and the game is quickly out of Kentucky's reach.

So the hunters begin packing and, every few minutes, another vehicle leaves the yard and heads out through the gate, onto the blacktop.

"I'll see you at the next hunt," one of the old members says to Joe Sewell on his way to the car.

"I hope so," Mr. Joe says. "It seems like all I do these days is bury my friends."

"Ah, hell," Wu Winslett says. "The next hunt is in a week. We'll all make it until then."

10

In the Shadow of a Giant

On Sunday—the last Sunday before the game—the sports pages around the state come to life. It is almost as if they woke up and realized there was less than a week to go before the big game. The coverage from now on will be intensive, nonstop, and nearly obsessive. No angle will go unexplored. No bit of color will remain unexploited. No cliché of sportswriting will be left unemployed. The sportswriters get just as cranked up for the game as anyone, even the players.

The *Tuscaloosa News* canvasses sportswriters around the state for their predictions. Auburn is heavily favored. The Montgomery paper runs a story about an Alabama player and his two Auburn sisters-in-law. "They wear these Auburn sweatshirts," he says, "and I don't even like to be in the same room with them."

Another paper begins a series on the great games in the series and the stars of those games. During the week there will be stories on the boys playing now whose fathers played in earlier games.

162

There will be stories on the ABC team of Keith Jackson and Frank Broyles when they arrive in Birmingham to cover the game. There will be predictions, analyses, and every possible angle will be exploited.

The coverage is nothing if it is not enthusiastic. But that, also, is part of the tradition here. The late Benny Marshall wrote about Alabama football games as if they were the modern version of the Peloponnesian Wars. He described the 1949 Auburn/Alabama game, which Auburn won in a tremendous upset, this way:

> For the players, it's close to war; for the fans, it's a party, and the Auburn football players—quiet now and tense—found festivity surrounding them as they climbed aboard for the crosstown trip. Some fans had begun the party early, and there are times when bourbon doesn't bring out the best in football fans. These happy ones . . . were waving fistfuls of bills and offering up bets as they approached an Auburn group.
>
> "Give you 25 points, kid. . . . Hey, War Eagle, this says you don't even score."
>
> Later some Auburn Tigers thought that this might have been the final firing-up they needed for the big game at the end of the season. . . . Auburn was a three touchdown underdog. . . . The prevailing opinion was that this Auburn team did not belong on the field with Alabama.

Sportswriters in Alabama are expected to be partisan—to be boosters, almost, of the sports, if not the teams, they cover. You can search the sports pages thoroughly for the sort of adversarial reporting that exists where coverage includes a professional franchise and never find it.

This does not mean the sports pages in Alabama are inferior. In fact, they are very good. The people covering sports care so much that it shows in their writing. Among the very best is Clyde Bolton, who has been doing it for a long time now, and can still make you feel the joy of sports. On this Sunday, his column is about high school football. It is addressed to the kids who are playing today:

What you can't know when you're spreading a thin coating of analgesic balm inside your teammate's jock is you will remember the horseplay 32 years later.

You high school football players of 1985 can't know that you will sit in the stadium 32 years later and close your eyes and see him at practice on that very field frantically undoing his pants and cussing his anonymous tormentor while everybody explodes with laughter and pleads innocence.

You can't know that 32 years later you will know so many plays.

You'll remember when you repeatedly blocked the all-stater who weighed 60 pounds more than you ever did.

You'll remember when you lowered your head and hit the defender at the goal line and scored the important touchdown in the opening game, and you'll remember your coach saying that was the best thing anybody did all night. Yes, you'll remember him saying that.

You'll remember intercepting a pass and being so excited that you ran over the back line of the end zone just to be absolutely certain you had scored.

But you'll also remember losing to one of your biggest rivals partly because a receiver caught a touchdown pass over you.

And you'll remember being as agile as a crosstie as a runner easily sidestepped you to score a long touchdown.

I've covered the Super Bowl and the World Series and the college bowls and the NCAA Final Four and the Indy 500, but I wouldn't swap standing in the dew at Valley Club Stadium on a Friday night waiting for an end-over-end kickoff to fall into my arms for any of those days in the press box. They have been great—but not greater.

Friday night I went to see my old high school, Alexandria, play Fairfield. I participated in the first game ever played in that stadium, as a junior, in 1952. I can't remember what I did two weeks ago, but I can remember that.

Lord how I envy those kids.

So, the sportswriting in Alabama is always a little more than professional or competent. It is done by people who know the state and football. What it lacks in urbanity or skepticism, is more than made up for in feeling and style. Consider this gem, from the lead paragraph about a high school football game, played years ago. The Banks-Woodlawn game was won, the story opened, on a last second field goal which "floated through the yearning arms of the uprights . . . truer than Tristan's love for Isolde."

Hard to beat that.

There is in all the state one exception to this rule about sportswriters. A single voice trying for some of the toughness that you find in other places where football is fair game for columnists.

His name is Paul Finebaum and he writes a column for the *Birmingham Post Herald*. Last year, he and Ray Perkins were near mortal enemies.

To understand their feud, it is necessary to know Ray Perkins—which is not easy—and to understand the kind of pressures he works under. And those are all too apparent.

When Perkins took the job, the line you heard, all around the state, was "Man, you don't want to be the one who follows the Bear. What you want to be is the man who follows the man who follows the Bear." Perkins, according to this consensus judgment, wouldn't last because he *couldn't* last. It just wasn't in the nature of things. The landscape of football was littered with the bleached bones of coaches who had tried to follow a legend. For a case history, you didn't have to look any further than Auburn, where Doug Barfield coached for five unhappy seasons after Shug Jordon retired. Barfield's great contribution to Auburn football was to make it possible for Pat Dye to come in clean. There were no ghosts haunting his every move. He was the man who followed the man who followed Jordon.

They told a story around the state, the first year that Perkins was there, about how his wife called someone in the neighborhood to complain about some dogs barking and disturbing her.

"Miz Perkins," the man who owned the dogs is supposed to have said, "those dogs was here before you got here and they're going to be here a *long* time after you're gone."

Perkins, though, did not plan on being a temporary coach. And if he didn't resemble the sainted man he was replacing in any of the superficial ways, he was his clone in the essentials. He was a fiend for work, almost frighteningly singleminded, and just plain country tough.

He came from Petal, Mississippi, outside of Hattiesburg. His father was a carpenter and small contractor. "We didn't have much," Perkins says, "but I never thought of us as poor." He began playing football in the seventh grade. He also began working after school, for extra money, at about that time. He liked the extra money enough that he quit school and started working full time at the gas station.

"I was just a wise ass. Thought I knew everything and nobody could tell me anything."

After a couple of years, he went back to school and football. He worked for the gas station in the mornings, before school, and in the afternoons, after practice.

He played fullback, but he was not highly recruited. Only Southern Mississippi seemed interested in him until Dude Hennessey, an Alabama assistant, came to town to look at another player and left more impressed by Perkins. Hennessey loves to tell the story of how he recruited Ray Perkins to Alabama.

"I went up to see him. I told him I liked the way he played and I wanted to buy him dinner. 'Can't go out to no dinner,' he said. 'First I got to practice and then I got to go over to the station and wash a bunch of trucks.'

"So I asked him if he could go out after he got through washing the trucks. He said, 'When I get through washing the trucks, I got to go home and study. And in the morning, I got to get up before school and go by the station and finish washing those trucks. Then I got to go to school. And after school, I've got to practice. And after practice,

I've got to go back to the station and wash some more trucks. So I haven't got time to go out to dinner.'

"He was the hardest recruit to spend money on I ever saw. I finally got him to go out to dinner one night. Him and his daddy. Took them to the best place in town. I was thinking about a five dollar, dripping red T-bone like you could get back then. We all sat down and the waitress came to take our order. Ray said he wanted the hamburger steak, well done. His daddy said he wanted the hamburger steak, well done. She got to me and I said, 'Give me the hamburger steak. Well done.' Whole dinner didn't cost me five dollars."

By the end of the season, Hennessey knew he wanted Perkins. He was fast and they loved speed at Alabama. Hennessey told Bryant about Perkins and said he wanted to offer him a scholarship. Bryant said all right.

When he told Perkins that he was prepared to offer him a scholarship to Alabama, Perkins took the news calmly. "He didn't go all to pieces or anything," Hennessey says. "He just told me he wanted to talk to the head man."

"So I said, 'When can you get to Tuscaloosa?' He said, 'There's no way I can leave here before four tomorrow morning.' I said, 'Fine. We'll see you over there in the morning.' I got back in my car and drove straight to Tuscaloosa and went to see Coach. I told him that Perkins was coming over in the morning to talk to him. Coach said, 'What's he want to see me about, Dude?' And I told him.

" 'Coach,' I said, 'he wants a married scholarship. He's in love with the English teacher.' Caroline Martin, Perkins's intended, was teaching at another school nearby. Over the years, she has become 'his teacher' in the telling of the story.

"Coach looked at me and said, 'Do you really want him?' And I said, 'Yessir, I really want him.' And Coach said, 'All right, Dude. I'll see him and I'll give him a married scholarship.' "

Bryant had given a scholarship to only one married player before Perkins. That was Lee Roy Jordan and some people say Bryant would have put him on scholarship if he'd had two wives.

So Perkins married the English teacher. They came to Tuscaloosa, where they lived in a small apartment converted from old World War II military housing, though during the season Perkins lived in the athletic dormitory with the rest of the players, according to team rules. He and his wife live a mile or two, geographically, from the spot now, though the material distance is vast, and the spiritual distance cannot be calculated. When Perkins arrived he was just one of nearly one hundred adolescent men brought to Tuscaloosa by Bryant, who would work them to see who would stay and play. Today, Perkins is one of the three or four best-known, most powerful men in the state. Which is why Hennessey likes to tell the story of that 98-cent hamburger steak.

Before he ever played a down for the varsity, Perkins was nearly killed playing football. He took a blow to the head in spring practice and walked around for a few days with a severe, blinding headache. He spent a night in the infirmary and, finally, was taken to a hospital in Birmingham where an examination revealed a subdural hematoma. Perkins says that when he heard that term, he was scared for the first time.

Doctors drilled three holes in his skull to relieve the pressure in his head. He was told to give up football but, of course, he would not do that. Bryant began telling people that Perkins had a steel plate put in his head and the story followed him everywhere he went. At Alabama, a reporter once asked Perkins about the plate.

"Never was one."

"No plate?"

"Nope."

"But all the stories . . ."

"Started by John Underwood in *Sports Illustrated*, 1967. Followed me ever since. They didn't have to put in a plate. All they did was drill three holes, here and here and here," he taps points on his skull with his index finger and when he does that, the reporter cringes a little. "That let the pressure off the brain and that was all there was to it."

"No lasting effects?"

"Seems like I got knocked out kind of easy from then on, but that was all."

He was redshirted for a year, meaning that he could not dress for the games, but he could practice. And that year would not count as one of the three years during which he could play for the varsity. (This was years before freshmen could play for the varsity.)

"Ray practiced as hard as anyone that year. Especially on catching footballs," Steve Sloan remembers. "He'd never been a receiver before, and he saw that's where he'd be if he was going to be playing for Alabama. So he got people to throw footballs at him, and gradually he learned how to catch the ball. He got to where he could catch anything you threw at him. By the time he started going into games as a receiver, he was just so reliable you knew that if you got it to him, he was going to catch it. I never saw Ray drop one in a game."

He was dedicated and he was tough. When he and Ken Stabler would pass on the practice field, a reporter from those days remembers, "Snake would look at him and say, 'Hi, Ray,' real friendly and Perkins would look back at him and say, 'Hi, sorry.' And he *meant* it."

Perkins had three great years. Two national championships and the year, 1966, when the team didn't win the national championship but was the only undefeated and untied major college team in the nation. He made All-Conference and All-American. He was drafted by New England in the American Football League and by Baltimore in the National Football League. He received a thirty-thousand-dollar bonus for signing with Baltimore and used the money to buy some three hundred acres of farmland outside of Tuscaloosa. This was 1966 and he paid less than one hundred dollars an acre.

"I must have known something, even then."

So Perkins left Tuscaloosa for the pros, hoping for a five-year career. Like Bryant, he believed you should have a plan for everything and five years was his plan. His coach at Baltimore was Don Shula, whose son would later start at quarterback for him at Alabama. "He never said anything about wanting to coach, but you knew it was there," Shula says. "He wanted to know about every phase of the game. He studied everything."

Perkins was a receiver, and he learned to watch film from one of the greatest, Raymond Berry. "He taught me how to watch film. I never knew how to study it before. Raymond does it better than anyone." Berry is also a head coach. His New England Patriots, to the surprise of almost everyone, would make it all the way to the 1986 Super Bowl.

At Baltimore, Perkins caught passes from Johnny Unitas and Earl Morrall. He played in two Super Bowls, including the 1969 game, which Baltimore lost to the New York Jets, whose quarterback, Joe Namath, had thrown passes to Ray Perkins at Alabama.

In 1973, when he tried to come back for a sixth season, he realized, and his coaches realized, that he couldn't do it. Injuries had finally caught up with him. His friend and teammate, Bill Curry, now head coach at Georgia Tech, remembers the day when Perkins knocked on his door and said, "Come on. Let's take a walk. I feel like I'm going to die."

"We all knew he couldn't play another year," Curry says. "Don McCafferty, who was our coach and who loved us like sons, was worried about Ray. He'd had three operations on his knee and, in our game against Miami the year before, he and Jake Scott had collided and Ray just lay there, out cold, for ten minutes.

"So Ray and I took a walk and I just told him that I understood what he was going through, but I knew that whatever he did next, he'd be a success at it. He said, 'I'm doing what I want to do, right now.' I didn't just say the magic words and make everything better. When he realized his football days were over, and we took that walk, Ray was inconsolable."

So Perkins retired and went back to Tuscaloosa, which

had been his off-season home all along. He'd worked in the real estate business, off-season. "And I liked it as long as I had football too." But when he tried real estate full time he knew he wasn't going to be happy.

"I came home one day and I told my wife that I wanted to get into coaching, full time. I quit my job and I started playing golf every day and calling people on the telephone, trying to find something in coaching."

It was not a wild impulse. He had been thinking about coaching since his days as a player and had once approached Bryant to ask his advice. "He told me I was crazy."

Perkins got a job coaching receivers at Mississippi State. After one year, he was hired by Chuck Fairbanks of the New England Patriots, where he stayed four years, again coaching receivers. Then he was hired by Tommy Prothro, who was head coach of the San Diego Chargers. He made Perkins his offensive coordinator, replacing Bill Walsh, who had been hired as head coach at Stanford University.

"Bear Bryant told me, a year or so before I hired Ray, that he was the best young coach of all the people who had played for him and gone into coaching," Prothro says. "And Ray was, and is, a great coach, in my opinion. He works very hard, but you see a lot of workaholics in coaching. Ray also has a way of working with people that makes them very loyal to him. The people who don't know him find a lot they don't like about him. The people who are close to him are *very* close to him. And I think that's a good thing in a coach."

Perkins's quarterback at San Diego was Dan Fouts and his offense set all sorts of yardage and scoring records that year.

People talked about Perkins as head coaching material. He held some conversations with Al Davis, the owner and chief executive of what was then the Oakland franchise of the Raiders, who have since moved to Los Angeles. Davis had a reputation as a football genius, a shrewd and nearly infallible judge of talent. He had enough regard for Perkins to consider him as a replacement for John Madden, who had been coach of the Raiders but who was leaving, exhausted and burned out.

"I finally called Al and told him I wasn't interested." The reason, Perkins explains, is that they were too much alike. They both wanted control and authority. "I knew if he offered it, and I took it, we'd have problems. I don't know that he was going to offer it. He did all right with the man he got, Tom Flores."

Perkins had been sounded out, then, by one of the best organizations in football. The Raiders are winners. Finishing high and going to the playoffs almost every year. The next team to contact Perkins had a different sort of reputation. The Giants were losers.

But they had a new general manager, who had been given wide authority by the Mara family, who had owned the team for years. George Young was a good football man, who had been with the Colts when Perkins was there and remembered him. When Perkins flew to New York to interview for the job of head coach, "I packed to stay. Because I knew I was going to get the job and I knew I could work with George Young."

The young man from Petal, Mississippi, had five years of coaching experience, four of it in the pros, when he took over the New York Giants. He was thirty-nine years old. Even Bryant said that he might be moving too fast.

Perkins took over a team with some of the most urbane, indeed *hip* fans in football. There had been a celebrated novel, called *A Fan's Notes*, in which the author described, vividly and brilliantly, the way the Giants became his obsession, his alter-ego. All sorts of people in communications and the arts followed the Giants passionately. Book editors who didn't care anything about sports, in general, would go out for lunch and talk about the Giants. A sports editor for the *New York Times* once told a writer who was working for him that, "I've done it so long now I don't care who wins or loses or what the score is, as long as the story is accurate. The only thing in all of sports that can still get my blood pumping is the New York Giants football team."

In the media capital of the world, the Giants were considered something of an institution by the press. It was as if the team belonged to them more than it did to the coach. And in a way, it was true. Coaches came and went, but the press stayed around, year after year. When Perkins got to New York, he seemed sometimes to be cultivating the antagonism of the press. He had a way of staring them down if they asked a question he either didn't like or didn't understand. Or, he might just challenge them.

"Coach, it looks like you're loaded at linebacker—"

"Now what do you *mean* by that?" he would say.

"Well, I mean, you've got Van Pelt, and Carson, and—"

"What do you mean by *loaded*?"

"Well—"

"You want to rephrase that question and then, maybe, I'll answer it."

Perkins made life so unpleasnt for the press that the beat man for one of the major New York papers took an early retirement. In the new regime, he said, it wasn't any fun anymore. By the end of his first year, the word about Perkins was that he "intimidated" the press.

"At first," he said, much later, "I was kind of proud of that. Little old country boy from Mississippi come up here and intimidates the New York press."

But Perkins was smart enough to recognize that he was making life hard for himself. And flexible enough to change. He met with reporters. After talking to them, he reopened the locker room and became more forthcoming at his press conferences. "I realized they had a job to do, same as I did."

By the time he left New York, he was respected by almost all the reporters and well liked by a few. And he felt like he'd learned something and been toughened, perhaps, in another way. Once, when he was under fire later at Alabama, he said he didn't let what reporters wrote there bother him because he'd been through it with the best and the guys who were writing about him now, "Couldn't load papers on a truck in New York."

Turning the press around was less important than turning the team around. Perkins came in tough. Players complained that he worked them too hard, so he got rid of some of them. The malcontents. And some who were using drugs. "He practiced addition by subtraction," one of the players said.

Some of the veteran players, especially, resented Perkins's rules and his system of fines and his policy of not playing a man who had not practiced during the week before a game.

"In my system, if you want to play, then you've got to practice," Perkins says. "That's the way it was when I was playing. How can you expect a team to act like a team, if the people who work hard all week sit on the bench on Sunday, while somebody else plays the game?" He benched All-Pros who wouldn't practice.

Perkins had losing seasons his first two years. In his third year, he took the Giants to the playoffs for the first time in eighteen years. (Watching on television as an overtime field goal got them there, one tough-minded, middle-aged book editor I know burst into tears.)

Parched Giant fans believed that Perkins was the agent of their deliverance. "He turned it around. They were losers. The worst kind of losers—the ones who *know* they are losers and think they deserve it—and he made them into winners. Some of it was selecting good players in the draft and some of it was good trading and some of it was luck, but a lot of it was good coaching," says a reporter who covered the team during those years.

Perkins had done what four other Giant coaches hadn't been able to do since 1963. Which is why the players and the fans were shocked, and even felt betrayed, when he quit while the next, strike-shortened season still had three games to run. The team, which had come around entirely to his ways of doing things, lost two games, much the way that Texas A&M had lost its last regular season games a quarter of a century earlier when its coach, Bear Bryant, had announced *he* was leaving to go back to Alabama.

The Giants won the last game they played under Ray Perkins as head coach, and though that victory was not enough to put them in the playoffs, or even give them a winning season, they carried him off the field on their shoulders. The Giants stumbled the first year after he left. But they were back in the playoffs the next two years and the people who follow the Giants faithfully still give the credit to Perkins. He was the one, they think, who turned it around. If he'd stayed, no telling how far they might have gone.

Harry Carson, the great Giant linebacker, agrees. "We were going in the right direction with Ray. He'd made us believe in ourselves and his methods. I think it cost us a year, at least when he left."

Perkins had been at Alabama less than one month when his boss died. He'd been hired to be head coach of the football team. Bryant was to have stayed on as athletic director. When Bryant died, President Thomas formed a search committee to find someone for the job. Perkins was on the committee and, very soon, he began to campaign for the job. Thomas, who understands the politics of football in Alabama perfectly, named Perkins athletic director.

"If I hadn't, and things had gone wrong, it would have been my fault. I'd have been accused of undermining his authority. This way, whatever happened, it was all on Ray's shoulders."

Perkins had won a power play, but he had made enemies in the process who were now waiting for him to fail. As troubles mounted during his first two years, there were those who said that the worst thing that had happened to him was the death of Bryant and that he never should have gone after the A.D. job. Others said no, it wasn't that. If he'd been losing, even Bryant couldn't have helped him. And he had to go for the whole thing. If he was going to succeed at Alabama, it was going to be all his way or not at all.

Perkins had so many problems in his first two years at Alabama that it is hard to say where they started. But if any one problem was symbolic of the whole thicket, then it was the matter of the tower.

By the time he died, most people saw a hound's tooth hat when they thought of Bear Bryant. But for people who went back with him to the beginning at Alabama, the symbol of Bryant and all of his methods was the tower. They say that he was the first coach to use one and that may be. Certainly it became part of the mystique that surrounded the man. "Coached 'em from a tower. Practice couldn't start until he got up there and the worst thing a player or an assistant could hear, during practice, was the sound of him coming down that ladder."

Jerry Duncan remembers how "he'd be in such a hurry to get down and get on somebody that he wouldn't even bother with the last few rungs of that ladder. He'd jump and he'd hit the ground running and you'd just be praying he wasn't coming after you."

Bryant watched all his practices from the tower. The players and the assistants who were running the drills couldn't look up so they felt his eyes were on them all through practice, even when the eyes were, in fact, on another part of the practice field. The psychology is self-evident. Also the fact that the man in the tower had better not miss anything. When you think about it, you realize that coaching from a tower would demand more of the man who did it than staying on the ground with the players. When you elevate yourself, you raise the stakes considerably and you give yourself that much farther to fall. Alabama fans loved the tower because Bryant was tough enough and mean enough to bring it off.

By the late seventies, the tower had gone from wood to steel and the old ladder had become a spiral staircase. The man who spent his afternoons in the tower didn't come down out of it as much as he had when Perkins and Duncan practiced in its shadows. But the tower still dominated the Alabama football practice field and to Bryant's followers it was to him what the corncob pipe had been to MacArthur or the plumed hat had been to J. E. B. Stuart.

Before his first spring practice, Ray Perkins had the tower taken down.

There were howls from Alabama fans. "You'd have thought he had taken the bones of a saint," said Rufus, the student of football and other important matters in Alabama, "and used them to fertilize his garden. It was a desecration, in their eyes."

Bad enough when the tower was left lying on its side in sight of the practice field. Worse, that after it was moved because it was distracting players, it was found lying on a flatbed trailer, rusting in the yard of a local steel mill. Perkins said simply it wasn't his style to coach from a tower and that he wanted the tower to be displayed in the museum portion of the Bryant complex. But three years into his tenure as head coach, fans were still phoning his radio show and asking him what had happened to the tower. Where was it now, they wanted to know, and would it ever be put someplace where people could look at it?

"There was no way Perkins could win on the tower," Rufus says. "If he'd climbed up in it, that would have made them even madder than taking it down did. Probably the only way he could have satisfied a lot of people on the tower was to go out there and put a lighted candle at its base every day before practice. Still, the way he handled it probably was insensitive. But hell, he's a football coach. He's supposed to be insensitive."

The next element in the combustible mix of changes made by Perkins was the firing of John Forney, who was almost as much a fixture on the Alabama football scene as the tower and was, furthermore, flesh and blood. "John was the human link that thousands of people had with Alabama football, and Bryant. He'd done the radio show for years. Done the Sunday television show for a while, too. He was a friend of Bryant's and he had hundreds of friends all over the state. They took it personally when Perkins fired him."

Forney was a visible man. An advertising professional who truly loved Alabama football, he did the games as a sideline. He also loved a party and a game of cards and he was known, around Birmingham, to put a dollar or two on the games he broadcast.

In the spring of 1980 Forney suffered a stroke. Bryant wrote to him in the hospital to wish him well, and when he had left the hospital for a rehab center one of Bryant's assistants came by. "Coach wants you to know," he said, "that the play-by-play job is yours whenever you're ready."

"That made me work harder," Forney says.

Then, sometime during the summer, Bryant himself came by. "You want some company," he grumbled, and sat down in a chair in Forney's room.

"I tried to talk just as plain as I could and after a while, he got up and said, 'Hell, you sound fine to me. I'll see you in September.' I didn't sound fine. But hearing him say that gave me something to shoot for."

The story of Forney's stroke and his comeback became widely known.

There were rumors that Perkins had some sort of change in mind for the broadcasting team. But before he could make a formal announcement and arrange a little ceremony of appreciation for Forney, Paul Finebaum broke the story. It was on the front page of the Birmingham newspapers. Though Forney and Perkins exchanged cordial letters and Forney even went so far as to write a letter which was published in *Sports Illustrated* saying that Perkins was within his rights and no hard feelings, there were many fans who took an intense dislike to Perkins over the episode. It struck them as unnecessary and ruthless.

So there were rumblings as Perkins started his first year. The tower . . . getting rid of John Forney . . . replacing most of Bryant's staff . . . changing sponsors for the television show—all moves he was entitled to make as head coach and athletic director. But moves that reminded Alabama people that Bryant was gone and also, by inference, called his judgment into question. Forney had been all right with Bryant, who'd said during a golf game after he'd retired that he wasn't going to make any changes in the broadcast team. The coaches had been Bryant's coaches. The sponsors had been fine with him. Perkins was rebuilding a program, some fans thought, that was in fine shape.

But people closer to the situation said the program was *not* in good shape. Discipline had crumbled and that was one reason Alabama was not getting the recruits it normally claimed almost automatically. There had been an episode in which an Alabama player had fired a shotgun in the direction of two students. And there was talk about drug use by some of the players. It was said that the shooting and the drug rumors were the real reason that Bo Jackson decided against Alabama. He had shown promise as a juvenile delinquent once and his mother, whom he listened to, wasn't going to let him fall in with that kind of trouble.

So Perkins instituted spot drug tests and tightened discipline. He also relaxed some rules. Players didn't have to sneak beer anymore, but they had better not be caught drunk.

At first, there was no arguing with the results. Halfway into his first season, the team was undefeated and ranked number four in the nation. Then it lost to Penn State on a disputed call. Alabama fans took the loss badly but rallied to Perkins. The next week, the team lost to Tennessee. The rumblings began again.

Late in the season, the team lost its third game, this one to Boston College. The rumbling grew a little louder, with Auburn coming up.

Auburn had a great team in 1983. Lost just one game, its opener, and was ranked in the top five. A victory over Alabama would put them in the Sugar Bowl, where they had a chance to win the national championship. It was a close, tough game and Auburn won by one point, 23–22.

Auburn went to New Orleans. Alabama went to El Paso

for the Sun Bowl, where they beat a good SMU team decisively. Auburn won and finished the season ranked third in the nation. Alabama fans were restrained but confident. Perkins had gone 8–4 in his first season. Which matched Bryant's record in his last season. The jury was still out.

Perkins himself seemed confident. He said, on several different occasions, that he was thinking national championship in his second season, 1984. This bothered the people who reflexively judged his every action by what they thought Bryant would have done. Bryant always downplayed his team's prospects. And the better those prospects were, the more he downplayed them. The worse Bryant poor-mouthed his chances, the more excited Alabama fans got. So when Perkins started talking national championship . . . a lot of them got worried.

"Everybody knew the talent was thin. He had some great players, but he didn't have very many of them. And the great teams these days are very deep," one of the Birmingham sportswriters says. "I still don't know if he was talking that way to build up the players' confidence, or his own, or if he really believed it. But it didn't take long for people to realize that he didn't have a national championship team."

Alabama lost its opening game, in prime time, to Boston College and Doug Flutie. The fans were tolerant because they understood that no amount of coaching could anticipate a quarterback like Flutie and because Alabama's fine freshman runner, Kerry Goode, ruined his knee in the game and would be out for the year. (And, it turned out, most of the next.)

Then Alabama lost its second game, to Georgia Tech. "It got very ugly, very fast. It was kind of frightening," the sportswriter says.

Alabama had not lost its first two games since 1956. The team beat Southwest Louisiana. Then, when it lost badly to Vanderbilt, in Tuscaloosa, on homecoming weekend . . . Alabama fans actually booed their own players and coach.

At this point Paul Finebaum, who had been hard on the team in his column, calling them "chumps" and "losers" published a poll inviting fans to rate Perkins and vote on whether or not he should be fired. "We have a circulation of 60,000. I guess we expected a few dozen responses. We got more than a thousand."

The local radio sports call-in show was humming with angry fans, calling to say they were ashamed and embarrassed by the way the Alabama team was playing. The story went around that someone had called in to Perkins himself, on his show, and asked, "Coach, how long would you say it takes to turn a college football program around?"

"About four years, I'd guess," Perkins answered.

"Well, congratulations, then, Coach. You done it in two."

Not all the stories were funny. Feelings were raw. *Sports Illustrated* sent Doug Looney to Tuscaloosa who, in his article, told of a dinner at Perkins's house where Finebaum had been the guest. The dinner had been arranged the previous summer, by Perkins's agent, with the idea of improving relations between his client and the press, in particular Finebaum, who had been tough on Perkins even before the disastrous season began. There were jokes around the state about Perkins. You could get a cold sitting next to the man, people said. They also said that if Perkins heard there was one man somewhere in the state who was still on his side, he'd call him up and say something to change his mind. Finebaum routinely printed that sort of thing.

So Finebaum had dinner at Perkins's house and they talked about their differences. Perkins said it didn't bother him what Finebaum wrote about him as a football coach. That was all fair game. But he objected to the stuff about his personality. "How can you write about my personality," he said, "when you don't even know me?"

"I agreed with that, more or less, and said so," Finebaum remembers. They sat down to dinner. Finebaum, Perkins, and Caroline Perkins. While they were eating, Perkins said that he was thinking about doing his television show with-

out a co-host. What did Finebaum think about that?
"I sort of sloughed it off."

Perkins asked his wife. *Sports Illustrated* reported "she
said, 'I don't think you have the personality for it.' According to Finebaum, Perkins crashed his fist to the table
and started ranting something about divorce."

The magazine called Finebaum twice before the story
appeared. Both times, he says, he asked them to either
take the business about divorce out "or at least make sure
people understood it was a joke. Because by then, I was
sure that he was joking. Sometimes, with Perkins, it's hard
to know."

A man who knew Looney well and also knew Perkins
and the situation at Alabama says he tried to argue Looney
out of using the business about a divorce unless he made
it plain that it was a joke. "Nobody who has ever been
around Perkins could think it was anything but a joke.
You've never seen two people who care about each other
more than Ray and Caroline. They have stayed together
through so much. That's a life that eats marriages *up*.
There is no way Ray would have said that . . . unless he
was joking. But when I told Looney that, he said, no,
Finebaum told him that it was said seriously."

Whatever . . . the story appeared. Perkins, who is a devoted family man, took it like he'd been blindsided. He
talked about suing. He called Finebaum a hatchet man
and he put pressure on the radio station that did his show
as well as Finebaum's to cancel the Finebaum show.

Finebaum says, "Perkins denies it, but I got it from
someone in his department. The station started leaning on
me to go easy on him and I knew it was a matter of time.
They canceled me after the season was over. In retrospect,
if I had it to do over, I would probably make some kind
of statement about the *Sports Illustrated* story. I didn't at
the time, because in that atmosphere, I didn't think it
would make any difference."

After the magazine article, there were threats on Finebaum's life. "I always got some pretty bizarre calls. But
during that period, it got really scary."

The *Sports Illustrated* story actually earned Perkins some temporary sympathy and gave the Alabama fans an outsider to hate. It was one thing for *them* to call the coach names . . . but when somebody from the Yankee press did it, that was a different thing altogether. That was just plain goddamned not to be tolerated.

For a while, things looked up. There was a victory over Penn State, and it probably helped that they were an Eastern team, coached by Joe Paterno, the favorite of the Yankee press.

President Joab Thomas issued a statement reaffirming his support for Perkins. "I knew he didn't have the material," Thomas says. "Coach Bryant had told me when he resigned that the material was there for one more good season and after that . . . he just didn't know."

In spite of Thomas's endorsement, rumors flew across the state like the flights of migrating rice birds. Perkins was going back to the pros. He'd been offered the head job at Tampa Bay and his house was already on the market. Several Alabama boosters had formed a group to buy out his contract and they were already talking to Danny Ford, a former Bryant player who had coached Clemson to a national championship. The "Jerk the Perk" slogan joined the currency of ordinary speech. A few people began calling Perkins "Ears" after the hapless J. B. Whitworth who had coached Alabama before Bryant arrived and was saddled with that nickname.

Alabama lost to Tennessee and LSU. Even before the Auburn game, it became certain that Alabama would have a losing season. Its first since 1957.

Perkins, through all of this, looked like the calmest man in the state.

Every Tuesday morning, he talked with his old friend Bill Curry, whose Georgia Tech team had beaten him earlier in the year. "He was fine," Curry says, "in fact, he kept reassuring me that he was all right, that he knew it was going to turn around and that he would just have to ride it out."

One of the men on Perkins's staff says, "I never saw it

get him down. You knew it was eating him up, but he never said anything and he never lashed out. After the Tennessee game, when things were just about at their lowest, he came in for a meeting and said, 'Okay, let's put that one behind us and start breaking down film for next week.' He was the one that kept us together. He showed real leadership during that time."

The Auburn game, when Bo Jackson went the wrong way, ended the season on a note of relief. Something had been salvaged. But a lot had also been revealed.

"Alabama fans are ugly," says the Birmingham sportswriter. "They're spoiled and they believe they have a right to win. They are terrible, childish losers. I remember when Alabama had been riding a winning streak that went twenty-eight games and they lost, finally, to Mississippi State. Right away you heard people talking about how Bryant ought to hang it up. He was too old to coach anymore. It made me sad, the way they were about Perkins and the team that year. But it didn't surprise me."

As for Perkins now . . . with only four days to go until Auburn, he says those problems are all behind him. It was tough, he says, but not nearly so tough as New York was. "I never want to go through anything like that again. It was so negative. Nobody thought you could win there. They expected to lose. At least here, people expected to win. They knew what it was like. Maybe they got a little complacent and last season woke 'em up. That way, it might be a good thing."

As for Paul Finebaum, he is predicting an Auburn win, by a close score, in his column, and saying in private that if Alabama does win, it will go a long way toward erasing the stain of last year's losing season. "All that other stuff . . . the business with the tower and John Forney and the assistant coaches, that will all be forgotten if he brings this team back. That's the heart of it.

"I think the real danger is that Auburn might come in all fired up and ready and be just too strong for Alabama.

Perkins has good players but no depth, and if he starts getting behind, and his defense has to play a lot, it could be a blowout. And then . . . he'd be right back to fourth and one, with his back to his own goal line.

"These Alabama fans only understand one thing, and that's winning."

11

Shug, Pat, and Bo

There is a joint press conference scheduled for Tuesday morning at Auburn. Pat Dye will appear first. Then Bo Jackson. Other players will be available around the cafeteria if anyone wants to talk to them.

Auburn is east of Montgomery on the eastern border of the state, in the region called "the plains." The school is much larger than the town and there is no mistaking that it is an agricultural and engineering school. There are research animals, crop fields right up to the borders of the campus, and buildings devoted to Poultry Science and Soil Dynamics. But it is a pretty school of red brick, grassy lawns, and lush oak trees.

There is no football complex at Auburn . . . yet. There are plans for one and ground will be broken soon. "But it won't be gaudy like that Taj Mahal they've got in Tuscaloosa," the visitor's guide says.

The visitor is met at the Coliseum, where Pat Sullivan's picture hangs in the lobby and his Heisman trophy is on

186

display in a glass case. There is time, the visitor's host says, to walk down to the stadium if he'd like.

It is a beautiful football stadium. Awesome in size and modern in appearance. The field is covered with thick natural grass. When the visitor remarks on this, his host says, "This is an *agriculture* school, my friend. There's no way we'd have artificial turf."

Auburn people are enormously proud of this stadium. When Coach Shug Jordan (he pronounced it Jerden) came to Auburn, the stadium seated less than 30,000 people, most of them in wooden bleachers. Under Jordan, the school's football program prospered and the stadium grew to its present size. Auburn people consider the stadium a monument to him and are proud of the fact that it has grown without any help from the taxpayers. The Bryant complex in Tuscaloosa, they are quick to point out, is being built with the help of state money.

This is the sort of injustice that Auburn people have grown used to.

Alabama people will counter by saying that while their athletic department has never taken a dime from the general state revenues, Auburn's has. The argument is endless. When you talk to people from one school it is as though your every word is being viewed in a mirror that reflects the image of the other school. A reporter from Birmingham saw Pat Dye one night at a reception. They talked and Dye asked the reporter where he'd been lately. The reporter said he'd been covering Alabama. Dye seemed interested and asked the reporter how Alabama was looking. When the reporter said he thought the team looked good, Dye's expression changed and he turned and walked away. "I'd ruined his evening," the reporter says. "I didn't say his looked bad. Only that Perkins's looked good. But that was enough."

The visitor asks about Shug Jordan. What sort of man was he? You don't hear that much about him outside of Alabama.

"No," his host says, "you don't. He was never much of

a self-promoter, if you know what I mean. He was a gentle-man. What he did, it was for Auburn and he made sure the glory went to the school and not to him. When one of his teams had a good season—and he had a lot of 'em—what you heard about was Auburn, not Shug Jordan."

If you want to know more about Shug Jordan, he says, you should talk to Jeff Beard, the former athletic director of Auburn and the man who hired Jordan, who was his friend, back in 1951. Beard still lives nearby, out in the country a few miles, on a farm where he and his wife raise Morgan horses.

Beard is only too happy to talk about Jordan. "Come on out," he says over the phone. "I'll tell you about Shug. Nobody knew him better than I did."

Beard is a tall man with a long face and jug ears and a wide smile. Most of what he remembers about Jordan makes him smile.

"Shug was born in Selma," Beard begins, "in 1918. Later on, when he was famous, he would go outside of the state to make talks and people would ask him where he was from and he'd say 'Selma, Alabama. Just a short walk from Montgomery.' A lot of them didn't get the joke.

"Shug was Irish and a Catholic. He went to parochial schools there in Selma. He was real proud and just as Irish as he could be. His grandparents were named O'Shaugh-nessy and you don't get any more Irish than that.

"He was left-handed and, when he went to school, the nuns made him learn how to write using his right hand. Later on in his life, he would go up to a blackboard and take a piece of chalk in each hand and start writing the same sentence in both directions. It was the darnedest thing. He said it was his only trick.

"When he was at Selma High, he lettered in football, basketball, baseball, and also in track. He graduated when he was sixteen and, like most of us then, he didn't have any money. So he went to work for the road department, on the highway crews.

"In those days, a lot of the little towns had baseball teams. There was one in Cottonhall that was run by the mill there. They paid Shug $1.50 for every game he pitched. I guess you could call it semi-pro. But in those days, we just called it lunch money. There were some pretty good players on those teams that you saw in places like Uniontown. Most of those kids couldn't afford to go to college, so playing for those teams was all they had.

"I grew up in Greensboro and it was so small that we didn't have a football team. Just basketball and baseball. I saw my first football game when I was in high school. I had a friend who owned an old car with no roof on it and we took it up to Montgomery to see some Alabama graduates play some Auburn graduates. In those days, you know, the two schools didn't play each other. So you had pick-up games like that one. I don't remember who won that day . . . so it must have been Alabama.

"Anyway, when we got to Montgomery, we ran into Shug—I knew him already from playing basketball against him—and a friend of his named Monk Morrison. Well, after the game, they had to get back to Selma. So we said we'd drive them. We had one hundred miles to go and not a foot of paved road. And after a while it started raining. Well, my friend had a pup tent in the car and we got that out and covered up with it and that was all right except pretty soon the pup tent started flapping against the muffler and caught on fire. We got it out, but we had a time.

"Anyway, Shug worked for a year on the road crews and I worked on them for a summer and we started Auburn together in 1928. In those days, you could register on credit and we did. Then we went looking for jobs. We both joined fraternities so we'd have a place to sleep. And we got jobs waiting on tables.

"Shug played center on the football team. He weighed one-hundred-and-sixty-five pounds. He was a great basketball player. He had a left-handed set shot that was just deadly. And he pitched for the baseball team. He went out for track and wanted to throw the discus, but the coach told him he didn't know how to coach a left-handed discus thrower and he'd appreciate it if Shug would just stick to baseball where they needed left-handed pitchers.

"There was a magazine back then called *College Humor*, that was real popular on all the campuses, and it wrote Shug up as an 'All-American Athlete' because he was a letterman—and real good—in so many sports.

"In 1932, Shug had stayed on at Auburn, even though he'd graduated. He was an assistant coach in football and basketball and then, after a couple of years, he moved up and took over as head coach of the basketball team.

"The head coach of the football team in those days would use Shug as his scout. That was before we started using film to study the teams we'd be playing next. I remember how he used to say to Shug, late in the week, 'Ralph, would you run up to Philadelphia and look at Villanova Saturday?' And Shug would have to go down to the bank to borrow money to pay for his train ticket. Then he'd get it back the next week.

"When World War Two started, Shug went into the army. He had a reserve commission in the engineers. He had to hurry around and get his uniforms before he went off up north somewhere—Massachusetts, I believe. And just as soon as he got up there, they put him on a boat and shipped him off to England. And he wasn't there more than two weeks before they had him on a troop ship heading for North Africa.

"He wrote me a long, homesick letter while he was on that ship. I've got it somewhere. Said he couldn't tell where he was going but that I'd know soon enough.

"He was in North Africa, Sicily, and Italy. He was in the Normandy invasion. Landed at Utah Beach. Somewhere in there, he got a shrapnel wound in his left arm. He wrote me about it and said that it wasn't much, but that it did ruin his fastball. He came back to the States after everything was over in Europe, but he didn't stay here two weeks until he was back overseas. This time in Okinawa. That's where he was when the war ended.

"I'll tell you one, now," Beard says, laughing. "It's about

when Shug was in the war. Show you what kind of football coach and what kind of person he was.

"Like I say, Shug used to scout for us and he was real good at it. Took the job seriously and worked at it. By the time the war came along, we had started using film so we'd look at that and use the reports Shug sent in from scouting a team. The year before he left, he scouted Georgia. This was when they had Trippi and Sinkwich in the same backfield. Those two made Georgia the best in the South and maybe in the whole country. But Shug had been scouting them for two years and, well, he'd found something. It was something that Trippi did with his feet to tip off whether he was going to run or pass. He had a play where he'd drop back like he was going to pass but it would be a fake. He'd pull the ball down and run with it. Shug found something that would let the defense know what he was going to do on that play.

"Well, the week before we were going over to Columbus to play them in 1942, Georgia beat Florida, 75–0. Just killed them. They were undefeated and coming off that game when we went over there. Shug was already overseas, but the coaches knew what he'd spotted and they were working with it in practice.

"So we played a great game and beat Georgia, 27–13. I think it is still one of the biggest upsets ever in college football. Georgia went on to the Rose Bowl, but that game liked to broke Wally's [Butts] heart. But Lord, did it make Auburn people happy.

"I took the film of that game and sent it to Shug over in North Africa. He showed it to a bunch of Auburn boys over there. And he took it with him to Sicily and Italy, and he still had it with him in Okinawa when the war ended. Then he brought it back to me and I still had it over in my office when I retired. I used to take it out and look at it every now and then. Still gave me goose bumps.

"When Shug came back from the war, there wasn't a place for him on the Auburn coaching staff. There should have been, since he'd been on some kind of leave of absence to fight the war. But he wasn't made welcome, so he coached for a year in Miami, as an assistant for a professional team called the Seahawks. They won some games, but they couldn't get anyone to come watch them. So they folded and Shug got a job with Wally at Georgia. He was line coach there and head basketball coach. He's probably the only coach who ever won a hundred games in both basketball and football.

"In 1948, Auburn needed a new head football coach. Shug applied for the job. But he didn't get it. They hired a boy named Earl Brown who was from Notre Dame. In those days, if you had you a coach from Notre Dame, then you were right uptown. It made Shug a little mad and he said to someone, 'If they don't have confidence in an Auburn man, then they ought to just close the place down.'

"Earl Brown was a good boy, nice personality, but he didn't know anything about coaching football. In his last year—that would have been 1950—we didn't win a single game. Lost to everyone. Even Wofford.

"We also needed a new athletic director. The man who'd been doing the job, Wilbur Hutsell, never wanted it in the first place. He was a trainer and a track coach and that's all he wanted to be. So one day he quit and the president, Dr. Draughon, who we all called 'Fesser,' said at a meeting, 'All right, who we going to get?' I said, 'I'm right here. You can get me.' I was business manager for the athletic department at the time.

"Fesser looked at me and he said 'Okay. You got it. Now go on back down there and run that place and don't bother me unless you get in trouble.'

"I didn't have much to work with in the beginning. We had to borrow money from the bank to meet the payroll until we could sell some tickets. And I knew that if we were going to sell any tickets, we were going to have to win some football games. I knew right off who I wanted to be in charge of that.

"I called Shug and told him Auburn was looking for a football coach. He said, 'I haven't applied.' I guess he was still smarting about being passed over that other time. I told him to just write a letter and that was that.

"In his first year, we went 5–5. His first game, we beat Vanderbilt and that was when they had Bill Wade. That was the beginning of the best years ever for Auburn football. The next year was tough. We went 2–8. But the year after that we went to a bowl game and that meant a lot more back then than it does now. Shug had put us on top and we stayed there twenty-five years while he was coach.

"Shug was a good recruiter because he was a country boy who hadn't changed. When he went into a boy's house to talk to him and his parents, well, they felt like they knew Shug. Like he was one of them and they could trust him. As a coach, he was the inspirational sort. He didn't do a lot of yelling and screaming and wouldn't kick a boy or grab him and shake him and yell at him in front of everybody. What he'd do was call him over. Just motion him with his finger, like so, and when the boy got over to where he was standing, Shug would throw his arm around him and start talking to him in a low voice about how he had to try harder and concentrate on what he was doing because all the other boys on the team were counting on him.

"He hated to discipline players. Hated it worse than anything. He'd put off doing it just as long as he could. I remember when we had a little quarterback from Atlanta—no point in mentioning any names—and that little devil just broke every rule there was. Nothing anybody said made any difference to him.

"Shug and I used to call each other Uncle Bob, and one day I said to him, 'Uncle Bob, how long are you going to put up with all this?'

"Shug said, 'I'm going to do something about it right now.' And he called the boy into his office and sent him home. Off the team. That meant we didn't have a quarterback. So Shug took a little old kid named Nix who had played some quarterback in high school and threw left-handed and made him his starting quarterback. Nix was quarterback on the national championship team and in the two years he was quarterback, he never lost a game. Tied one.

"Shug had a way of getting his boys to go out and *play* for him and they all loved him. They'd come back all the time. They always knew they could talk to him.

"Of course he loved Auburn. This is where he wanted to be. He got calls from other schools and a couple from the pros. But he always told them he wasn't interested. He didn't get the newspaper attention that Bryant, over in Tuscaloosa, got. But it never bothered him. Shug and I used to laugh about it and say that it would ruin Paul's whole day if his name wasn't in the papers—good or bad, didn't make any difference just as long as he was in there.

"Shug was a private person, even though he liked people. He'd go home and have lunch with his wife and he liked to be home after work in time for the six o'clock news. Seems like he was always doing something around the house. He did some gardening and he always had tomato plants he was real proud of. He read a lot. He read history. He liked reading about the Civil War.

"We used to fish a lot in the early days. Just get a bunch of crickets and some cane poles and go. But after a while we didn't do so much of that. Seems like we got busy. I do remember a time when we were out here at one of these lakes and we got on a bream bed and we were just bringing them in. I said, 'Shug, we got a meeting of the athletic committee in thirty minutes,' and he said, 'Oh the hell with 'em.' And we stayed on fishing. Only time I ever saw him do anything like that. Nobody ever said anything about it.

"I tried to get him to play golf and he did for a while, but he never really cared anything about it. I guess what he liked best, next to being around the house and coaching his boys, was going out and speaking to some Auburn people somewhere. He was real good at that. And after he got through with his speech, he would sit around visiting with those Auburn people. He truly enjoyed that.

"He retired in 1977. He probably should have done it earlier, like I did. I retired in 1972. But Shug wanted to put in twenty-five years. He was real sick at the end. He died of leukemia, you know, and right there at the end, he just got so tired that he couldn't keep his eyes open. But he died at home. In his sleep.

"He touched a lot of lives and there just isn't any way of saying how much he did for Auburn. Everything he did, he did for Auburn. He didn't do it for himself or to get his name in the papers. He did it for Auburn. He *loved* Auburn. He truly did."

Back at the football offices in the Coliseum, the visitor learns more about Jordan. When he retired, he was fourth in total victories among active coaches, with 175. He was first diagnosed as having leukemia in 1968 and he barely survived. In those days, sportswriters from across the South took what was called a "Skywriters Tour" of all the Southeastern Conference schools. When they got to Auburn, they were shocked at the appearance of Jordan, who was one of their favorite coaches. Finally, one of the reporters couldn't stand to leave the subject alone any longer. "Coach," he asked Jordan, who was behind a podium, doing his best to answer questions about the coming season, "Coach, are you *dying?*"

Jordan's jowled face never flinched. He studied his questioner for a while and then said something about how he'd survived four invasions during the war so he considered every day a blessing and tried to get the most out of it. That was something he believed in.

"And," he went on, "let me promise you that if I *was* dying I'd sure as hell find a better way to spend my last days than answering a bunch of questions from you people."

The writers loved him. He was good with his answers. One of them asked him which he preferred, one-platoon or two-platoon football.

One platoon, Jordan answered, because that way, if some skinny little halfback fumbled the ball on his own five-yard line, he had to stay out there and keep the other people from scoring with it.

He was a gentleman, and if he felt any bitterness over

the unfair and inevitable comparisons to Bryant, he never went public with it.

When you consider his achievements, it is impossible not to wonder what he might have done if he hadn't coached in a state where the other school had the most successful program in the nation.

"He brought Auburn to where it is today," the man in the football offices says. "Before Bryant went to Alabama, Wallace Wade and Frank Thomas had already been there. The tradition started with them. Here, the tradition starts with Shug Jordan."

And continues, perhaps, with Pat Dye. Auburn fans devoutly hope so and Pat Dye is doing all that is humanly possible to make it so.

Dye looks weary and harassed when he comes into the room where the reporters are waiting. He sits at a large walnut desk; behind him, there is a large blue flag with AUBURN blazed onto it in orange letters. Dye leans down into the microphones and says, quietly, "Well, it's that time of year again."

He has a way of speaking that makes a sentence rise quickly and then fall off slowly so that by the time he reaches the end of a thought, you are straining to hear what it is he has to say, even when it is so predictable that the reporters in this room could have written it without leaving their motel rooms. Bryant's famous growling/mumbling way of talking accomplished the same thing. It made you listen even when the words weren't very important.

"We've got tremendous respect for Alabama and the great job their coaches have done. The closest team we can compare them to is Florida. I don't know how good we are. I really think that on Saturday, we'll find out. Alabama's going to be as good as they can be and I believe we will be too. So I think we'll find out if we're average or if we're really a good football team."

The reporters carefully write all this down and then one asks, "Coach, did last year's game hurt recruiting?"

Dye is too much the fundamental farm boy to lie, so he gives the man an evasive answer. "Well, some have their minds made up before you even play the game. It's hard to believe that just one game can have that much of an effect on recruiting. I doubt if it has much effect out of state." He pauses, touches his hair, and then says, "What did Ray say about it?"

"He said it didn't have any effect," several reporters answer in unison. Dye nods. Nobody in this room believes that. Perkins was merely proving that he'd learned something about press conferences in New York.

"Coach," somebody asks, "do you think about the last few minutes of last year's game?"

"No," Dye says, "not at all. I guess I'm fortunate not to be very smart. I can't think of but one thing at the time and right now I'm concentrating on this year's game."

Dye is a favorite with the reporters. Probably the coach they like best in all of the South. He is great company off the record, at night, over a couple of beers. So they lay off now. He looks tired and his eyes are bleary; he has had a cold for days. After one or two more questions, Dye thanks everyone, stands up, and leaves the room.

Then Bo Jackson walks in and sits in the chair where Dye had been sitting. The wire service and out-of-town reporters come to life. This is the leading Heisman candidate and all season long he has been bringing big city talent into Auburn. The *New York Times* has been here. *Sports Illustrated. USA Today.*

Jackson looks big and explosive, even sitting behind a desk. Knobs of muscle show plainly through the fabric of his shirt. His shoulders are wide enough so their slope is graceful and his chest is both broad and thick, tapering into a high, narrow waist. You can't see the legs, now that he is sitting, but when he walked into the room, they were the first thing you noticed. They are thicker than fence posts above the knees and you cannot imagine the defender strong enough to wrap his arms around both those legs when they are moving and bringing this man down.

He has a pleasant face. Smooth and unblemished. Patient eyes. An overall expression of shyness. The uncomfortable look of someone who is doing what he has to do but would much rather be somewhere else.

"How you feeling, Bo?"

"Feel great." This is the biggest press conference lie of the week but that won't come out until much later.

"Leg one hundred percent?"

"It's almost there," he says, softly.

"Do you think much about last year's game and the play?"

"No, I don't think much about it."

"You think you got a bad rap, Bo?"

"No. I didn't get a bad rap. I did go the wrong way. But if I had gone the right way, we still might not have scored. They were as pumped up as we were."

"What about the Heisman, Bo?"

"Well, I'll think about that after the Alabama game."

He speaks very carefully, making sure of each word, as though he might have some sort of speech problem that only this kind of concentration can overcome. Or it could be his shyness. Whatever, it makes him that much more appealing. Even vulnerable, though what he does best in the world is run over people just as big as he is.

Somebody asks if he and Cornelius Bennett, the fine Alabama linebacker, are friends.

"Yes," Jackson says, "I knew him in high school and this past spring we went to Miami together to get our pictures taken for the Playboy All-American team." This is one of the things that makes this game what it is, the visitor thinks. So many of the players know each other. Might have grown up friends and teammates through high school. The opposing fans are neighbors. Even the coaches know each other in more than passing fashion. When he left Tuscaloosa for his first coaching job, Ray Perkins had to get rid of a pickup truck. He sold it to Pat Dye.

"Bo," one of the reporters asks, "what about the game itself. Do you think too much is made of it?"

Jackson works even harder with the tiny muscles of his mouth—no doubt the only muscles in his body that give him trouble—to answer this question. It is a thoughtful answer. "I think some people do make too much out of it. No matter who wins, we both still represent the state."

Somebody asks if he has been getting any extra harassment as the time for the big game draws closer. "I get some hate mail, but I don't read it. I know when it's hate mail because it won't have no outside address on it. So I just throw it away."

There are no more questions. When Jackson stands to leave a reporter calls out, "Good luck, Bo."

Later some reporters gather in the cafeteria of the athletic dorm to talk to other ballplayers and among themselves.

Much of the talk is about the game. Reporters have no better line on that than anyone else. But they are also talking about the Heisman and *that* they understand perfectly, since it is the press that casts the votes.

"I hear *Sports Illustrated* has a cover that says neither Bo nor Long should win it," one reporter says.

"I've seen the piece," another says. "It's brutal. Really brutal. Does everything but call Bo an outright coward. Says he spent more time on the bench this season than Sandra Day O'Connor."

"Cheap shot."

"Maybe. But a lot of people read the magazine."

"Let me tell you something about Bo Jackson's guts," one man says in a little heat. "Last year, against Texas, he dislocates his shoulder, right?"

"I remember, sure."

"Well, he ran three more plays before he even said anything to anybody. That man has all the guts in the world. Don't let that soft-spoken, meek-as-a-lamb act you saw today fool you. That's off the football field. Between the sidelines, he's tough as they come."

"He'll have a chance to prove it on Saturday. Show the whole country."

"And I'm betting he will."

In another conversation, a reporter says, "Old Pat looks wound pretty tight, doesn't he?"

"He's looking at the biggest game of his coaching career."

"Um hum. And he's probably wondering which one of his teams is going to show up. The one that beat Georgia or the one that lost to Florida."

"I saw Perkins yesterday, in Tuscaloosa. He looked like the coolest man in the state. Like whatever happens on Saturday, it doesn't make any difference to him. You think he knows something?"

"He might. You know, I'm beginning to think he actually might be a good coach. Even a great coach. If he wins this game, I'll be convinced. Because on paper, there's no way he should win."

"You know, you'd probably have to go back to '71 to find one of these things where they were so evenly matched and there was so much on the line. That was the year they were both undefeated."

"I know. And Sullivan won the Heisman."

"But Alabama won the game. In a blowout."

"This won't be a blowout."

"No. But I'll tell you what it's going to come down to. It's going to come down to Bo Jackson. He's going to be on national television, running for the Heisman, against his team's greatest rival. He's never had a bad day against Alabama and I think he's going to have a great one on Saturday. And that's going to be the difference."

"Makes as much sense as any other prediction."

"How would you like it if *Sports Illustrated* said you didn't have any guts?"

Bo Jackson has given more interviews in four years than he can possibly remember. He is the biggest thing on the Auburn campus. Reporters came to the press conferences to hear what he, not Dye, had to say. For anyone who knows the state well, this is still startling, even in 1985. Jackson, after all, is black. Twenty years ago, no blacks played for either Alabama or Auburn. In fact, neither school scheduled any teams with black players.

Now, the best football player in the state, and probably the nation, is black. And playing for Auburn.

After the season, when he was again giving individual interviews, Jackson says that no, that wasn't something he ever thought about. He'd never gone to a segregated school.

"I think people in Alabama still have a long way to go," he says. "White people and black people. Some of the old people in the state just won't let go. Everything is still 'nigger' and 'honkie' to them. The young people are better."

The visitor thinks, as he drives away from Auburn and passes through one small town after another on his way back across the state, how much Bo Jackson was fortunate to miss.

There is a young man in one of these towns who will be going to Auburn next year and may even start at defensive back. He is black, and he was recruited by Notre Dame and Texas, but he decided on Auburn because he didn't want to leave home. Before he went to Auburn, Bo Jackson had only been outside the state of Alabama once in his life. That was to go to an amusement park near Atlanta, called Six Flags.

That young blacks from Alabama do not want to leave the state, that they would rather stay and play for Alabama or Auburn so that they can be near the small towns where they come from—that they choose to stay when they could so easily escape—that is something that would have seemed a miracle one biblical generation ago.

That has changed so much while the towns have remained. Waverly. Camp Hill. Dadeville. Alexander City, where Red Phillips, Auburn's All-American receiver from the '57 national champions, still lives. Sylacauga, home of big Jon Hand, the defensive tackle on this year's Alabama team. Childersburg.

The names of the towns are a kind of melody to both Alabama and Auburn fans. The pre-game introductions, when the announcer calls off the home town of each player, is a kind of music.

This year's rosters list players from Alabaster, Opp, Theodore, Maplesville, Flomaton, Thorsby, Leeds, Atmore, Nostagula, Valley, Red Bay, Town Creek, and Elba.

So you can look at the roster and know that the players are from Alabama. That much is for sure. But you won't know if they are black or white without a picture. And there was a time, not so long ago, when you didn't need that.

If they didn't still play this game in late November and the towns weren't still there, every few miles along the highway, you could say that this state had changed entirely. But the towns are still here and they still play the game. In three days time.

12

Fans on Wheels

On Wednesday, with the game still three days away, some fans from other parts of the state begin to arrive in Birmingham. Especially the fans who come in their motor homes. They need to come at least one day early to find parking close to Legion Field. By getting here today, they are assured of a good spot.

Motor homes are a new element in football. Before they became popular, fans would drive to the game and stay in a hotel, unless they were from close by. The motor home owners drive to the game *in* their hotel room, which is actually better than the kind you'd get at a Holiday Inn, since it has a bar and a kitchen and you can walk from the front door to the football stadium in less than a minute.

Motor home owners decorate their vehicles in the school colors, paint the school name on the sides and over the spare tire cover, and rig the horn to blow the first few notes of the school fight song. Before a game, they stock the bar, fill the refrigerator, top the tank, and hit the road. There are Auburn fans who have taken their motor homes to every game this year and Alabama fans who've been to all the games except Penn State. The motor homes do not get very good mileage. If you take one much farther than North Carolina, the fuel bill can mount up and pass what it would cost you to fly and stay in a hotel.

As the motor homes pull into the parking lots around Legion Field, people greet each other. The Auburn people will know other Auburn people, just as the Alabama people will know other Alabama people. But here, at this game, there will be Auburn people who know Alabama people strictly from having parked next to them for this game in past years. In fact, among the tribe of motor home fans, there is a sort of rough camaraderie that prevails right up until game time, when the Auburn people go and sit on the Auburn side of the field and the Alabama people go and sit on their side.

Parties and cookouts begin almost as soon as the first motor homes pull in and park. As the lot fills, people walk through the ranks of parked Winnebagos and Vikings and all the others, looking for people they met at last year's game. When they find them, they hug and congratulate each other on a good season and argue about where to go for a drink—your motor home or mine.

Tomorrow is Thanksgiving, and many of these people will cook the turkey in a microwave in the motor home kitchen and have family dinner right there in the shadow of Legion Field. Some will have teamed up with other families so that one microwave can be doing the turkey while another does the casseroles.

On game day there will be a one-man band, playing out of the bed of a pickup truck. At least there has been as long as any of the motor home fans can remember. He is an Alabama fan, for some reason, but everyone is invited to dance to his music after the game. Usually the winners dance more than the losers, who sit in front of their motor homes talking softly and drinking.

"No other way to go," a man who owns one of these motor homes says to a visitor. "All the comforts of home, including a television. You can watch the pre-game show and then get up and walk over to the stadium in time for kickoff. Most of us don't, though. We go in early with the rest of them."

The visitor wonders if there would be any point to the motor home without football games to drive to.

"Probably. But it wouldn't be the same."

Would he go to football games if he couldn't go by motor home?

"Probably. But it sure wouldn't be as much fun," he says. "But if you'll come with me, I'll introduce you to someone who wouldn't see any football games at all if it weren't for one of these things."

He leads the visitor across the lot to another rank of motor homes. Knocks on a door, and when someone steps out, introduces the visitor.

The woman the visitor is introduced to has been in kidney dialysis for almost ten years. She goes to every Alabama football game, always traveling by motor home. "I can't ever be more than three days from a machine," she says. "And normal travel is awful tiring. But in one of these, I can rest."

She is an Alabama fan and disappointed that the team will be going to Hawaii to play in the Aloha Bowl. Any other bowl game, and she and her husband could go in the motor home. But, she says smiling, there isn't any *way* you can drive one of these things to Hawaii.

And she doesn't like flying, the visitor asks.

No, she says, she doesn't mind it. It's not as nice as traveling by motor home, but she doesn't mind it. The problem with flying, especially on a long flight, like to Hawaii, is that the airplane might get hijacked. And if it took them longer than three days to work out a deal, she'd be dead.

Both Auburn and Alabama send their students home for Thanksgiving and, as each campus empties, a vast low pressure area covers the state and dismal cold rains fall on the last full-speed practices. Auburn practices inside, on a covered field. Alabama does not have a covered field yet. Perkins keeps his team outside, running through its plays in the rain.

The weather becomes a topic of intense interest now. Rain should favor Auburn, the bigger team with the better running game. That, at least, is what everyone says. Auburn is the favorite of most writers and all bookies. The betting line is three and a half points. But they say that some local bookies are giving more points to generate some action on Alabama.

That night several men sit at Michael's, a downtown Birmingham restaurant, eating red meat and talking about the game.

"That three-and-a-half-point line kind of surprised me," one of them says.

"Why is that?" says the visitor.

"Oh, down here it doesn't make any difference what the line is, there will always be some action on Alabama. I've seen the line go to thirty points and people would still be betting on the team. They wouldn't think of betting *against* them, even with those kind of points. I've heard bookies say that Alabama fans are the worst bettors he's ever had the pleasure of dealing with. When it comes to the Tide, they always bet with their glands."

"And you know," says Rufus, who is at this dinner, "it wouldn't make any difference to this game if there was no line, no betting. I don't believe you can say that about professional football anywhere in the country. A lot of people bet on those games so they'll have a reason to be interested in them."

"That's right," the other man says. "Down here, they're already interested. More than interested. I think they bet because they figure as long as they've got their hearts and souls on the line, they ought to put some money down too."

"Absolutely," Rufus says, "and a stupid bet is even better than a shrewd one—taking the points and hoping Alabama's opponent will cover, even though Alabama wins. See, when you make one of those stupid bets, you're saying you don't care about the money . . . what you care about is your football team. And if somebody, somewhere, thinks they can't win by more than thirty, well, hell, you'll take a piece of that."

So what is at the bottom of it, the visitor asks.

"It's a fight," Rufus says happily. "A feud. It's not polite to admit, but people *like* a good fight. A real old-fashioned, country ass-whipping. Clears the soul and gets the blood moving again the way it's supposed to.

"This is a great big fight between the two biggest clans in the state. Your best against our best. And it's for nothing but pride. There's a lot of money changes hands and there's people, like the coaches, who make a living off it. But it's not about commerce. It's about pride and a good fight and a lot of other irrational things. Hell, the whole thing is irrational and that's the joy of it.

"It's irrational for a bunch of boys to work as hard as the players do, to suffer the kind of pain and exhaustion they do, just to play a game for free. Most of them will never make a nickel—not an honest one, anyway—playing football. That's part of the beauty of this thing. That's why we love it.

"People from up north look at us and they give it the old patronizing shake of the head. Not grown-up and mature. But look at them. What do they have that gets their blood pumping like this? The lottery is about the only thing. Otherwise, it's all orderly and rational. You work eight hours and you don't work any harder than you have to. You eat right, don't drink too much, get plenty of sleep, sign up for life insurance, take some adult education, take out an IRA . . . and you see if you can't squeeze all the juice out of your life.

"This is a *fight*, man. A real head-knocking, snot-slinging, eye-gouging fight. People get excited. Get drunk. Howl and raise hell. Remember that they are Celts—the fightingest, most clannish people to settle this country. This isn't the sideshow, it's the best part of life. That's why it is so important."

13

Thanksgiving

The visitor spends Thanksgiving Day at Big Oak Boys Ranch, not far from Gadsden. He has been invited up by John Croyle, who played for Alabama in the early seventies and who passed up professional football for something he wanted more. Croyle is one of many football players who found a way to reconcile religion with their violent, profane game. But then, the Army of Northern Virginia was full of practicing Christians and, between battles, the soldiers preached to one another and conducted revivals.

Big Oak looks more like a raw, unfinished suburban development than a ranch. There is a gate and a small one-story frame building that serves as an office. Then, down a gravel drive, there are four two-story brick buildings where the boys in Croyle's care live.

"I want them to grow up thinking they live in a normal, middle-class neighborhood," Croyle says.

Eight boys live in each house, along with house parents. The boys range from six to seventeen years old.

"We look for private placements," Croyle says. This generally means that the boys are brought here by one parent or another. Or by a grandparent or an aunt or uncle. "If I've had 360 boys come through here," Croyle says, "then 359 of them have come from broken families. What kills you are the boys we get who have been brought here by parents, abandoned after they've been abused, and they still want to go home. They still love those parents and they blame themselves for whatever has happened. You wouldn't believe some of the things that have been done to these boys. I've got one, his mother dunked him in a tub full of scalding water because he was crying. There's another kid here whose face is palsied and his eye wanders because his father hit him so hard. I've seen them with bones broken and teeth knocked out. Sexually abused. Neglected. It's hard to believe, even after you've seen as much of it as I have."

Croyle started Big Oak after he finished at Alabama in 1973. He was a defensive end who played in the famous "punt, Bama, punt" game against Auburn and the next year in the Sugar Bowl against Notre Dame, another famous loss.

"That was going to be our year to win the national championship," Croyle says. "And we almost did. Last I remember of that game, we were winning."

The visitor waits for an explanation.

"Do you remember that game?"

A little bit, the visitor says.

"Well, you remember how they had to hold it up for about ten minutes in the fourth quarter because there was an unconscious Alabama player on the field?"

Oh, yes, the visitor says.

"Well, that was me. When I woke up the next day in a New Orleans hospital, I was ready to go back in. But we'd already lost."

Croyle is an intensely—though not oppressively—religious man. "I've found something that works for me," he says. "I'd *like* to share it, but I'm not going to force it on you."

The decision between professional football and the kind

of work that he does now was a spiritual decision for him. Being knocked cold in the Sugar Bowl was a kind of sign.

"I'd been thinking about pro ball just as a way to raise money to do this. After that game, I decided to go ahead and do this and to have faith that the money would be there."

The earnest money for the purchase of the land came from John Croyle Day in Gadsden. The people of the community wanted to honor one of their own who'd done well in football. It happens commonly around the state. Once a boy graduates, it is legal for him to accept gifts. His neighbors wanted to give Croyle a car.

"I told them I really appreciated the thought, but that I'd rather have the money. That gave them a jolt, but when I told them what I wanted it for, they understood. So I got a $5,000 check.

"That left me about $45,000 short on what I needed to buy this land and get started. I got fifteen from a doctor who knew what I was doing and wanted to help. Then John Hannah—you remember him, big All-American at Alabama and an All-Pro now with New England—well, he was involved in a situation where he would get a bonus if he came to summer training camp. There was some kind of walkout going on, but John didn't believe in it. John calls me and he says, 'Whatever my bonus is, you can have it.' Well, it came through on the last possible day and it was for $30,000. I had my place."

One of the red brick buildings where the boys live is called the John Hannah House. Another is named in honor of Bear Bryant, who gave, over the years, nearly $70,000. A third is named for someone whose name has no connection to Alabama football. "Just good people," Croyle says. The fourth is named for Ray Perkins, who donated the $60,000 it cost to build it.

"Actually, I traded him a horse for it," Croyle says. "I'll trade anything that can't talk. I'm always looking for ways to raise money. One horse for one building seemed like a good deal to me."

Croyle wants to raise enough money, eventually, to build

a total of ten of his houses and a gym. "I know a gym sounds like a luxury, but you've got to be around here sometime when it's been raining for three days and I've got thirty boys who've been inside the whole time."

It has been raining all Thanksgiving morning, but the boys are willing to sit still for a turkey dinner. They all wear Levi's, running shoes, and T-shirts, and they look about as American as it is possible to look. One six-year-old boy fills his face with turkey and talks to the visitor between bites.

"You know who Ray Perkins is?"

"Sure do."

"Well, you know what I got?"

"What's that?"

"I got a football that he wrote his name on and then gave it to me."

"No kidding."

"Nope. You want to see it?"

"Sure."

The boy starts to push away from the table and the house mother says, firmly, "After you're finished eating."

"Yes, ma'am."

This boy, the visitor learns later from the house parents, was brought to the ranch by his mother, who, after being beaten for years by her husband, divorced and went back to school to study nursing. She decided she just couldn't handle both raising the boy and going to school. The boy calls the house mother Mom and the house father Pop, but he still cries some nights for his real father and mother.

"You must be pulling for Alabama then," the visitor says, "when they play Auburn on Saturday."

"You bet I am. And we're going to beat 'em, too."

"No, you ain't," says the boy who is sitting next to him at the table, wearing an Auburn T-shirt. The boys are both six and, according to the house mother, best friends. The boy with the football signed by Ray Perkins is white and the boy wearing the Auburn T-shirt is black. His mother is a prostitute.

"Auburn's going to kill 'em. Bo Jackson is just going to run all *over* Alabama. You watch and see."

"No, he won't," the other boy says.

"Yes, he will."

"Do you know big John?" the first boy says to the visitor.

"You mean John Croyle?"

"Big John, yes, sir. Well he used to play for Alabama and *he* could stop Bo Jackson."

The other boy won't argue with that.

The older boys are quiet. Either from shyness, the visitor thinks, or because they are old enough to be thinking the kind of thoughts that come to you on Thanksgiving when you are not with your own family.

"It was delicious, Mom, can I be excused?"

"Yes."

"Delicious, Mom, can I be excused?"

"Yes."

The big boys leave the table, carrying their dishes into the kitchen. Two of them will clean up after the meal. Everyone draws chores, which are rotated week to week.

The two six-year-olds take the visitor upstairs to show him the famous autographed football and a few other treasures. The rooms are neat and the beds are made. There are the usual posters and pennants on the walls.

Because the sky has temporarily cleared, the boys all want to go outside and the house parents are only too happy to oblige them. The older boys are interested in riding the three-wheelers around the ranch grounds while the younger boys want to go fishing in the pond.

The visitor gets the tour. There is a small herd of Angus-Hereford crossbreeds in a lower pasture. A few saddle horses. A swine operation not far from the fishing pond. All of this is aimed at making the ranch self-sufficient. "But I don't believe it is possible to raise as much as thirty boys eat," Croyle says, "not even on two hundred acres."

So Croyle solicits money and any other kind of help he can get. "I'm always looking for contributions," he says.

"Any way I can get 'em. If somebody has got something that he wants to give me, I'll go pick it up. We had a tornado here, couple of years back, tore up the meat lockers at a local grocery. All that meat was going to spoil if somebody didn't take it. You want to bet I didn't go in with a truck and get every bit I could carry and bring it back out here.

"We get stuff from everywhere. We got a swimming pool came from a guy I'd never met. He'd been in jail, where I'd gone visiting, and later on when he got out, and his life had turned around, he decided to do something for us. He had a construction company by then, so he built us a swimming pool.

"I'll take any donation and I'll do anything for publicity. I use the recognition that playing football for Alabama gave me, and I use it for all it's worth. I go to the golf tournaments. I get athletes out here. We had a race car driver out here one time. I didn't know anything about him, somebody had brought him up because he was down in Talladega for a race and thought he might be interested and want to help us out. Well, he was asking me what we needed here, most of all, and I said you wouldn't believe how fast a boy can knock the knees out of a pair of blue jeans. Well, wouldn't you know that he was sponsored by Wrangler Jeans. So, who says the Lord doesn't provide?" Croyle smiles a huge, slightly manic smile when he says this. When he starts talking about his ranch it sometimes seems like he cannot talk fast enough to say it all.

And the visitor, like everyone who comes there, is profoundly touched. Especially on this day, when he is away from his own family. He manages to ask, in some form, the question everyone who visits wants to ask, which is . . . why?

"I don't know. I guess I learned something early in my life. My sister and I were at a funeral and we had slipped away from everyone else. I was 4 and she was 5. We weren't interested in all that praying. We were playing on some tombstones, climbing on them, and I walked away a little piece and then I heard something, and when I turned around, I saw that the gravestone had come loose and fallen down on my sister. She was crushed underneath it.

"My father got it off her and we put her in the car and were driving to the hospital and I was looking at her. I said, 'Daddy, she's turning blue.' And he said, 'She's dying, son.'

"I guess I learned then that life isn't all fun and games. Everything else followed from that."

And what, the visitor fumbles to ask, is it that he can give these boys? That he most wants to give them?

"Well . . . love, of course. You can't believe how much some of these boys just need to be hugged. I've got a callous around my waist from all the hugs. They haven't had much of that before they got here. Not the kind of love where they know it's always going to be there. They've never had that before. I tell 'em that I love 'em and I'm always going to be here. And I guess on top of that, I try to provide these boys with a strong male role model. Somebody who will stand up to them, discipline them when he has to. I know people think it sounds mushy, but anyone who ever played football for Coach Bryant understands the importance of that. He was the authority figure for all of us who played for him. The reason we didn't quit, why we played as hard as we could, and the reason we succeeded. These boys have never had anyone like that in their lives. Too many people in this world never have."

The sky closes and comes lower again and the rains return. The boys come back inside, muddy and tired, one of them with a stringer of a dozen crappie he caught in the pond. The house father helps clean the fish.

The boys either watch television—the Dallas Cowboys are soundly beating the St. Louis Cardinals—or go off to their rooms to read or listen to the radio. The visitor says goodbye to all of them and promises the one six-year-old that he will say hello to Ray Perkins for him and tell him that the boy still has the football.

"Tell him I'll be pulling for him on Saturday, too."

For sure, the visitor says. Before he leaves, he asks John Croyle if he is going to the game.

No, but he'll be watching it on television with his wife and things will be loud and interesting.

Why is that?

"Because she went to Auburn," Croyle says, "but I love her anyway."

14

Counting Down

On Friday they start pouring into Birmingham and filling up the hotels and motels, most of which have been solidly booked for weeks. Their cars trail crepe streamers in the school colors and have "War Eagle" or "Roll Tide" soaped on the rear windows. Some of the fans are dressed in the school colors. This can be done discreetly—an orange-and-blue rep tie is fairly distinguished looking—or it can be done gaudily. In the lobbies around Birmingham, you see it both ways.

One man checks into the Hilton, where the Auburn team will be staying, dressed in blue pants, white shirt, blue tie, and an orange blazer. His shoes have blue tassels and, probably, his socks are orange. When he sees a friend across the lobby, he shouts "War damn Eagle."

"War damn Eagle," the friend shouts back and after the formalities of checking in are done with, they retire to the downstairs bar, which is already crowded with people wearing orange and blue and shouting "War damn Eagle."

"I'm confident that we're going to win the game to-morrow," one of the men at the bar says. "But right now we got to reach way down, suck up our guts, and win the party tonight."

"War Eagle."

Yeah.

Out at the Sheraton Perimeter, the scene is more or less the same, except the colors are more subdued. Crimson and white don't announce themselves like orange and blue. But the mood here is high, though not quite as high as it is across town at the Hilton. You hear the occasional "Roll Tide," and see people check in and then go off, arm in arm, for the bar, where the noise level climbs by the minute.

By every estimate, Alabama fans are more subdued than Auburn fans. There are theories to account for this. One is that Alabama people are stuffy and reserved and behave pretty much the way you would expect a bunch of bankers and lawyers to behave. That is, needless to say, an Auburn theory.

Another theory is that Auburn people are just hot blooded and excitable and don't know how to behave any other way. This is an Alabama theory.

A less partisan, more abstract theory is that Alabama fans got so used to winning that it no longer means as much to them. The thrill isn't the same. Auburn people have never known that feeling.

To the visitor, both sets of fans seem plenty passionate. And the stories he hears just confirm it.

There is one about the group from South Alabama, three men who came up to the game every year. One was an Alabama lumber man. Another was an Auburn veterinarian. The third was an Auburn man who worked for the state. They were friends. Had been for years. Hunted and fished together.

In 1972, as they got ready for the drive, the veterinarian was especially loud about how this was going to be an Auburn year.

"I can feel it. I can just feel it. Old Beah may be undefeated, but we got a bunch of little boys going to change that. After tonight, old Beah ain't going to be undefeated no more."

He kept it up, for the four-hour drive to Birmingham and all through the pre-game drills and ceremonies. Alabama scored first, scored again, and was holding Auburn to five yards total offense in the first half. The vet grew quieter and quieter and then, at halftime, excused himself to go to the bathroom.

He never returned. He missed the entire third quarter and the fourth quarter as well, when Auburn finally kicked a field goal and then, in the last five minutes, blocked two punts and ran them both in for touchdowns to win the game.

The vet's friends assumed, at first, that he had just gone out to wait for them in the car, but when they got there, they could find no sign of him. They waited by the car for an hour, thinking that maybe he'd been caught up in the excitement with some other Auburn fans. Gone to a party at one of the motor homes, maybe. But finally, when the parking lots were empty and it was long since dark and they were still waiting, the man's friends got worried. They called his wife in South Alabama to see if maybe he had been arrested for something, or had gotten in some kind of trouble.

"He's right here," his wife said when she answered the phone. "Been here for the last hour, sitting in the dark, drinking bourbon. He got so upset watching the game that he left the stadium and got a ride to the bus station and caught the Greyhound all the way home. He hasn't said a word since he got here. I've seen him take it pretty hard when Auburn loses a football game, but I've never seen him like this before."

"Well," one of the other men said, "you can tell him to turn on the lights. Auburn won the game."

The visitor hears stories about a man who shot his wife for switching television channels in the middle of an Alabama game. Stories about people who have refused to go to weddings that were held on the same day Alabama and Auburn played—that would have to be an out-of-state wedding since there are *no* weddings in Alabama on the day of the game.

Stories about a man who had gone to school at Alabama during the Ray Perkins–Ken Stabler years and had kept on going to the games year after year and who, during the losing season, two years ago, would sit up in the stands with tears running down his face. Stories about the Auburn boy who came home to Birmingham on the weekend of the game and was full of charm and good spirits and a delight to his parents but who, after Auburn had lost the game on Saturday, did not say another word until late Sunday afternoon when he loaded his car and said simply, "Goodbye," before driving back to school. Of how, in the Sunday papers after the game, most years, you will see a story about how a fight got started over the game in a honky-tonk somewhere and wound up with somebody dead on the floor. Of how one or two people every year die of a heart attack right there in Legion Field. The better the game, the more who die.

As the city fills with excited, passionate fans, the stories begin to sound perfectly natural. Women with tiny blue tiger tracks painted on their cheeks look normal. So do men wearing huge crimson cowboy hats with "Roll Tide" embroidered on the crown. You don't wonder at the sight of a box of Tide laundry detergent propped up in the rear window of an automobile and flanked by two rolls of toilet paper. (Roll, Tide, Roll—don't you see?) The excitement that seemed a little strange and immature in the morning has become a magnetic and palpable thing by late afternoon, and you find yourself watching the front door of the hotel to see who is coming in next. You feel the rising tension in the knot of fans waiting in the lobby for the buses carrying the team to pull up outside. You listen in on conversations between men discussing the Auburn pass rush as against Mike Shula's ability to scramble as though what is being said is important and that, by eavesdropping, you might actually learn something.

In short, you catch a little of the fever yourself.

The Alabama team arrives to great cheering and much autograph signing. Shula, who is a quiet, good-looking kid with a lot of chin, just like his father, is surrounded by young girls who look at him the way girls look at rock stars. Fans spot favorite players, boys from back home where they've come from, and yell greetings and encouragement.

"David, David!"

"Hi, Mr. and Mrs. Scott."

"Play hard, David, we'll be pulling for you."

"Thank you. We will."

Perkins and the coaches shake hands and have their shoulders and backs slapped repeatedly by men who just want to say they saw the coach last night, "and he looked good. Real good. *Confident,* you know."

Perkins and the other coaches smile and thank their supporters. After a few minutes of such confusion, all the players and coaches go up to their rooms and the lobby is almost quiet again. The crowd thins a little, but many of the people will not leave because they know that in an hour or two the team will be coming down again, to eat in one of the banquet rooms and then have one last meeting. So they'll wait to get another look at their players and coaches and to give them a few more handshakes and shoulder pats and words of deeply felt encouragement.

It is the same at the Hilton.

"Go, Bo. Run *over* those sumbitches, you hear, Bo. Don't stop at two. Run that thing for three hundred yards."

"Tracy, hey, Tracy. Put it to 'em now, son. Knock their eyes crossed."

"We love you, Pat."

"Waaaaaaaaaaaaaaaaaaaaaaaaaaaaaaaaaar Eagle!"

There are parties everywhere in town. In rooms at the hotels and in motor homes down by Legion Field, where people run from one machine to the next, through the cold rain, to invite its occupants over.

"We know you're Auburn, but we'd still like to have you come by."

There is a huge "Beat Bama" party at the Civic Center, where at least a thousand people dance to the music of the Drifters. Some of the people here are in their fifties, and some are in their twenties, but most are baby boomers, members of the Big Chill generation, dancing to the background music of their best memories.

There are people eating and drinking all over town and talking up the game.

"Hard to imagine," one man says, "what it would take to shut this party down. Maybe if the President got shot . . ."

As you stand on the sidewalk, waiting to cross the street, a car comes by and the windows all go down simultaneously and four voices shout "Rooooooooooooooooooll Tide!"

You will hear that cry—and its opposite, Waaaaaaaaaaaar Eagle—through the night, and into the early morning when you'll wake up in a strange hotel room and listen to the sounds around you, remembering where you are. There is the sound of light traffic outside. The sound of the rain. The hum of the hotel heating unit. And, from time to time, the sound of a human voice, or several human voices, raised in ecstatic war cries.

You realize as you listen to the sound—Rooooooooooooooooll Tide—that you will be forever disappointed if you look for a kernel of rationality in all of this. Like Rufus said, it is the sweet soul of irrationality that utters those cries. Nobody came to town tonight because it makes sense. They came because it is in their genes to choose sides and fight. This is Celtic blood and four generations of learned behavior. This is howling done by people who love to howl. This is one day when none of that other stuff—IRA's, crop rotations, school board meetings, prostate surgery, alimony, and termites—none of that means a goddamned thing. This is a night—and a day after—to howl and to let your blood have its due. So the cries echo down the hallways. *Rooooooooooooooooll Tide. Waaaaaaaaaaaaaar Eagle.* And you lie in bed and listen with the flesh popping on the back of your neck, wondering if this is what they sounded like when . . . oh, when they came out of the woods at Chancellorsville. Nobody knows what it sounded like, but it has to have sounded something like this. And if you were a Union soldier who'd just stacked arms and was cooking supper, the sound would have terrified you.

After a while, you go back to sleep. The howling goes on, you imagine, until dawn.

15

The Game

The sky was still heavy on the morning of the game and the rain fell until nearly noon, when it stopped entirely and the sky cleared to a clean, blinding blue. The air was cool and the temperature was probably in the low sixties. There was a slight breeze. It was a beautiful day for a football game.

There is no parking to speak of around Legion Field, so the people who live near the stadium—most of them black and living in what used to be housing for the steel mills which have now closed—sell space in their yards and driveways. You pay anywhere from three to fifteen dollars, depending on how close you get to the stadium.

The same people who rent parking places often fire up a charcoal grill in the front yard and cook up a mess of bar-b-que, which they also sell to the fans. They will even rent you the use of their bathroom.

Some do-gooder in the city health department has been trying to get the sale of front yard bar-b-que outlawed. And once he accomplishes that, he will probably find a way to make it illegal to rent out your bathroom. But today the people who live around Legion Field are doing a brisk trade in parking space, bar-b-que, and bathrooms.

There is no alcohol sold inside Legion Field, and it is supposedly illegal to carry in your own supply. But outside the stadium, in the beauty of this fall day, there are dozens of cocktail parties in progress. Especially around the assembled motor homes.

The visitor is welcomed by a family of Auburn fans and a cold beer is in his hand almost before he can refuse the offer.

"Go on, we got plenty. And don't ever say that Auburn folks aren't friendly and generous."

There is fried chicken. Potato salad. Cole slaw. Ham. All manner of good things. Also a mood of high anticipation. "Oh, there'll be some head busting going on out there today. It's just going to be a war."

The visitor meets a woman named Patsy, who is a devoted Auburn fan. She and her husband take the motor home to all the team's games. She sends boxes of fudge and cookies and other treats to the boys at the dorm. A couple of years ago she sent a poster that was a collage of photographs to Lionel James, Auburn's great runner now with the pros, and he liked it so much that Patsy now makes them up for several players. "I had to because Bo stole Lionel's poster. I told him, I said, 'Bo, if you want a poster just *ask* me for one. I'll make it for you.' "

Patsy and her family are confident. And after he has drunk their beer and eaten their chicken, the visitor wishes them well.

"Come back after the game and help us celebrate."

The visitor says he'll do that.

The stadium is filled, every seat, long before kickoff. The fans are cheering and hollering their "Roooooooll Tide"s and "Waaaaaaar Eagle"s until the din makes it hard to think and to resist the wave of emotion. Better to ride with it.

When the Alabama team comes out on the field, one of the big men who will be playing on the offensive line all afternoon vomits from the tension. A teammate asks him if he is all right and he doesn't even answer. Merely stares out at the field.

On both benches, before the kickoff, the players are shouting and pounding on each other. Yelling encouragement and trying to give vent to some of the pressure. An Auburn player holds his helmet in one hand and hits it repeatedly with the other. He is hitting the helmet hard enough that it would hurt in normal circumstances. But now, he doesn't notice.

After the kickoff, the ball changes hands twice. But Alabama looks sharp and Auburn looks tentative. On Auburn's first play from scrimmage, Bo Jackson gets the ball, as expected, and tries the middle of the Alabama line where he is gang tackled and stopped after a yard or so. Along the Alabama bench, players shout, "Hit him, hit him," and pound each other's shoulder pads. They all know that Jackson will carry the ball at least another thirty times, unless he gets hurt. Still, this is a good way to start. On Auburn's second possession, Bo is stopped on third and short and along the Alabama sideline the feeling of confidence begins to grow. Maybe *this* year, they'll stop him.

Auburn kicks Alabama deep into a hole. Mike Shula, his composure draped around him like a cloak, comes out throwing. He hits Al Bell for a long gainer on second down. Then hits him again. He throws three consecutive completions and begins to look unstoppable. Relaxed and in charge, he hands off to the fullback who turns and pitches the ball back to him. Shula throws another completion. He is four out of five. Alabama is driving and Auburn is scratching to stop them. The Alabama side of the field is rocking. Alabama scores from in close when the fullback carries. The kick is good. 7–0.

Auburn takes the kickoff and when quarterback Pat Washington drops back to pass, John Hand wraps him up and the ball is loose. Alabama recovers the fumble but can't move. Van Tiffen kicks a field goal. 10–0.

Auburn has no drive. Nothing. The team seems heavy-footed and thoroughly unsure of itself. Bo is gang tackled when he tries the middle and when he goes outside, the defense strings him out, containing him until he either reaches the sideline or the pursuit catches up with him.

Dude Hennessey, retired for several years before Perkins invited him to stand on the sidelines with the team, shouts "This game is in the bag." Hennessey has no coaching responsibilities. He is there to fire up the team. He paces up and down, shouts, and exhorts. He kicks and spits and shakes his fist. He gets mad and he yells just like he did for Bryant, in the years when the man he recruited for a ninety-eight-cent hamburger steak was out there catching passes. Hennessey does wear a headset. But he is not connected to the coaches in the press box. He is listening to the radio broadcast of the game.

Auburn punts and Alabama returns for sixty yards. The punter makes the tackle. He has had surgery for a club foot and he must be the slowest man on the team . . . but on this play, he is fast enough and gutty enough.

Alabama can't move and kicks another field goal. "They don't believe they can win," an Alabama player shouts to his teammates on the bench. "They don't believe they can win."

The ABC reporter on the Auburn side of the field says the players there are "in shock." Alabama fans are booming out their cheers and the Auburn fans are quiet.

"We should be getting touchdowns," Darwin Holt says. He is standing on the Alabama sideline at Perkins's invitation. He is still a great supporter of the team, a driving force behind the "First and Ten Club," which helps Alabama players find careers after their playing days are over. Holt is as excited now as he was when he played. He pounds shoulders and when he sniffs out the play, he hollers, "Pass, pass," as though he were still a linebacker, trying to alert his teammates.

"We should have scored touchdowns," he says. "You can't be satisfied with field goals when you play these people. You *know* that their big guy is going to break one sooner or later."

Sure enough. On Auburn's next possession, Washington

completes a 47-yard pass to get Auburn down close to the Alabama goal line. From inside the ten, Washington puts the ball in Bo's stomach and he runs straight up the middle, breaking over two defenders at the two-yard line and into the end zone, for a hard-earned touchdown.

This is the lift Auburn needed.

On the extra point, Big Jon Hand hurts his knee. He is on crutches on the sideline during the kickoff and shortly after that, leaves for the dressing room.

Alabama is stopped. The kicker with the broken leg punts fifty-eight yards.

Bo runs one twenty yards through the middle. Then, on a four-yard carry you can hear the thud of his body from the sideline as he collides with an Alabama linebacker; he bounces off, with his legs still driving, and tries to get more. *Uh huh huh*, the sound comes from his mouth as his legs pump and he looks for a moment like he is going to break it, but the one hit has slowed him enough that the rest of the defense has time to crowd in and bury him in a pile.

Another long Shula completion to Al Bell gets Alabama close enough to score three more points or another Van Tiffen field goal.

But with time running out, Auburn moves on two long completions. On one, the receiver takes the ball over the middle and gets hit twice, hard, before he goes down. A sack pushes Auburn back. With time running out in the half, they kick a forty-nine-yard field goal, longest of the year for the Auburn kicker. The teams go to the locker rooms with the score 16–10 Alabama. It has been Alabama for one quarter and then Auburn for the next. Auburn has played almost fifty men while Alabama has played only thirty. Everyone knows that Alabama lacks depth. Alabama will have to go with the same men at almost every position for the rest of the game. It looks like Auburn's game to win.

Up in the press box, reporters eat the fried chicken and country ham with biscuits that have been laid on by David Housel, Auburn's enormously able sports information director. "Hell of a game, isn't it?" he says to an out-of-town reporter, as though he were responsible for providing that, too.

"One of the best I've seen," the reporter says. "You've got to wonder if they can keep up this pace next half."

"Oh I don't believe they'll have any trouble," Housel says. "I don't believe that'll be any trouble at all."

The judgment in the press box is that Alabama came into the game better prepared than Auburn, but that now the superior power and depth of Auburn will carry the second half and win the game.

"But it's a dogfight," one reporter says. "Just like everyone expected."

The third quarter is scoreless. After each series, the Alabama defense comes to the sideline and sits together. Cornelius Bennett, the star linebacker, drinks from the oxygen mask. Another linebacker sits slumped, looking at his feet, as though trying to conserve his energies and his concentration for the moment when he will go back on the field. Jon Hand, back on the field, holds ice to his knee and grimaces.

The hitting is audible all over the field. Players come off on the Auburn side holding their elbows or a knee, then shake their heads to show they are all right. Nobody wants to come out.

The sun falls behind the Birmingham skyline and the dome of blue changes to an intense violet with large flocks of migrating blackbirds moving across it. The noise inside the stadium seems to rise as the sun goes down. You can feel the stands shaking. The third quarter ends with the score unchanged and the outcome still in doubt. The noise in the stadium seems to rise like the wind ahead of a storm.

With three minutes gone in the fourth quarter, Auburn takes the ball deep in its own territory. This is basically a power running team that has not moved the ball on the ground all day long. The first play of this series looks like more of the same when Bo is stopped after picking up a couple of tough yards.

But his next carry is good enough for a first down. Reggie

Ware, another Auburn back, gets ten more. Bo gets another
ten. He makes another one of those tough inside runs,
breaking two tackles and taking an Alabama linebacker
head on and planting him with the impact.

Tommy Agee, another big Auburn back, picks up a first
down.

Now the Auburn offense looks strong and inevitable. The
Alabama defense looks tired, like a game boxer whose legs
have finally gone. Bo has run over a hundred yards and
he is just beginning to look like the most dangerous runner
in the country. He takes the ball, starts right and then goes
back to the left when he senses the hole is there. Another
first down.

Agee up the middle for a first down.

Then Cornelius Bennett breaks through and gets a sack.
Second and nineteen. Then third and still nineteen.

Big play. The fourth quarter is running down. This should
be the climax of the game. If Alabama can stop this drive,
then it should win the game.

But Bo Jackson takes a little dropoff pass and carries it
almost all the way in.

First and goal at the six. The fans have reached another
pitch and the noise is continuous.

Jackson picks up two.

Alabama holds on second down.

On third, Pat Washington takes it to the half-yard line.

So, will it be Jackson over the top? Or will Jack Crowe
call a sweep, like he did last year, and will Bo miss the
signal?

Keith Jackson, doing the game for ABC, says, "The Auburn offense has worked so hard, if they don't get it here,
then what's left?"

It's true that the game feels that way. There is some
time left in the fourth quarter, but the game has been hard
and long and this feels like the moment. Each team will
summon up its best effort now. Whoever is stronger should
win.

This year the call is for Bo over the top. He makes it,
but just barely. The Auburn bench erupts. Players and

coaches pound on each other and shout, "That a way, Bo. That a way, *Bo*." Auburn kicks the extra point. 17–16. At this moment, it feels like Auburn has the thing won. Alabama has not made a long drive since the first quarter, and Alabama does not have a Bo Jackson. This is the first time Auburn has had the lead but the Auburn fans yell to the skies because, in this game, once should be enough. Less than seven minutes are left when Auburn kicks off.

Alabama makes a shallow return of the kickoff and has some eighty yards to go against an Auburn defense that has gotten tougher by the quarter and now has a lead to protect. If they can get the ball back, get it to Bo, then the big man will run right at them, until the clock runs out.

Then, on a routine toss play, the basic bread and butter running call, Gene Jelks, the freshman halfback, breaks through the line and cuts upfield. Before the Auburn defense, which is overshifted, can recover, he is racing for the goal, coming by the Alabama bench with his head thrown back, his eyes bulging, and the cords in his neck straining so that they show through the skin. He is snorting as he runs, like a race horse, and he makes it all the way to the corner of the end zone without being touched. The whole Alabama bench, including Perkins, mobs him. Shula goes for two. No good. 22–17, Alabama.

Now it seems that Alabama should win.

Two long drives into the teeth of the Alabama defense in the last quarter of this game . . . that seems like too much to ask. Even of Bo Jackson in the last regular season game of his career.

While the teams line up for the kickoff, Big Jon Hand stands in front of the Alabama defensive unit, saying, "They ain't going to score again because to score again, they got to go over me. And they *ain't* going to go over me." He still limps from the first-half injury but he is 6' 8" and 280 and an All-American. The strength of the Alabama line.

After the kickoff, the Auburn offense has seventy yards to go and some five minutes left in the game.

They start the way they had to start. Bo Jackson for four

tough yards. A rare pass takes Auburn twenty yards to its own forty-five. Then Jackson carries for a couple . . . Jackson for five or six. By now, even he looks tired. But everyone else looks tired, too.

Washington picks up six or seven. Jackson hits for five. On a sweep, Jackson is forced out of bounds and an Alabama player gets called for a late hit. This stops the clock.

Jackson gets it down to the one-yard line with one minute left to go in the game.

This time, Reggie Ware takes it in. The two-point attempt fails. With a minute left, it is 23–22 Auburn. The second drive was tougher on the players and the fans than the first. It was nothing but football. The fundamental game. The same game Bryant and Jordan coached. Except for the substitutions . . . it could have been "eleven men and sic 'em."

On the Auburn side of the field, Bo Jackson stands on the bench waving a white towel in circles over his head, urging the Auburn fans to cheer louder and louder.

"I think the good Lord is going to punish him for that," Dude Hennessey says. "I just don't believe He'll allow an athlete that great to hot dog it."

There was still hope on the Alabama side. In the first game of the year, Shula had taken his team the length of the field with less than a minute to play to beat Georgia. He had done it to tie SLU. He had nearly done it against Tennessee in one of the two games Alabama lost.

But this is Auburn. Perkins and Shula consult. It is a close call as to which is the coolest. Probably Shula. He stands with the slight slump that seems the mark of great Alabama quarterbacks—the Namath slouch—and listens to what his coach has to say. Then he turns and runs onto the field at a jog that is so relaxed it could be just another day at the office.

Down at the Alabama end of the field, Dr. Joab Thomas stands with his arms folded across his chest, watching, dismayed as Shula drops back on first and ten and throws . . . incomplete.

On second down, he drops back again and looks for a receiver. They are all covered. He tries to move around and buy some time but the Auburn rush is strong.

"Throw it, Mike. *Throw it,*" Thomas and thirty or forty thousand other Alabama fans shout.

But Shula cannot get rid of the ball and is sacked for an eight-yard loss. Alabama calls its last time out. Thirty-seven seconds left to play.

Shula goes to the sideline again. Comes back on the field, calls his play, then takes the snap and drops back again. He waits until his man comes open and then he throws. Complete, but still short of the first down. Fourth and two. Twenty-three seconds left in the game. One more play for the Auburn defense. Stop this one and it is all over.

Shula takes the snap, drops back, and then, instead of passing, hands off to Al Bell, his receiver, coming around on a reverse. For a moment, the play looks like a bust. An Auburn lineman has sniffed it out and is closing in on Bell as he makes his turn. But Shula throws a hard block and Bell goes for twenty yards to the Alabama forty-six before he steps out of bounds to stop the clock with twenty-one seconds left.

Dr. Thomas hollers, "Nice block. That a way, *Mike.*"

Shula throws one incomplete. The noise is deafening now. Legion Field seems to throb like an overheated engine.

Shula drops back. The blocking holds. He throws across the middle and the receiver catches the ball and runs out of bounds at the Auburn thirty-six. There are now just six seconds left in the game. The Alabama field goal unit comes on.

It seems almost quiet now. On the Auburn bench, Pat Washington hides his eyes.

The ball is snapped and Auburn puts on a hard rush. Van Tiffen, who was three weeks ago being called a "disgrace to the University," steps into it and kicks. The ball rises against the white glare of the lights and then floats down between the uprights true as a rifle shot.

The Alabama fans stayed in their seats cheering for forty-five minutes after the game.

Outside the Auburn dressing room, the players come out one by one, still wet from the showers, holding their over-night bags in one hand and a small box of fried chicken in the other. The chicken is for the bus ride back to Auburn.

Pat Washington, the Auburn quarterback, comes out and a red-haired woman gives him a hug and tells him it is all right, that he'd done all he could and they love him. Washington is dry-eyed but the woman is crying.

A lot of the Auburn players are crying, though. One big lineman comes out, so plainly exhausted that he can hardly walk, and tries to get on the bus. But he can barely raise his foot, so he stands there for a minute, leaning against the door, sobbing.

An Auburn fan reaches out to touch him and he pulls away, steps up into the bus, and finds a seat somewhere in the darkness.

A few Auburn fans stay by the bus, patting shoulders and muttering a few words of support and encouragement. Then, when the buses are full, they drift off to the parties that are already in progress at the motor homes parked around Legion Field.

"This one hurts even more than last year," Patsy tells the visitor when he drops by to say goodbye.

Down the line a man is climbing up on the roof of his motor home to fix his television antenna. Out of the dark-ness a voice shouts, "Hey, there's an Auburn man going to commit suicide. Don't do it, buddy. Don't jump. There's always next year."

People laugh.

The one-man band is playing hard from the back of the pickup truck and people are clustered around it, dancing.

The game is over, but the celebrating has just begun.

16

Another Sunday

Sunday morning, Ray Perkins is up early. He drives to the studio where he tapes his show. Hergert leads in with the winning kick and it is still a thrilling moment in the dim light of the studio as it rolls across a half a dozen different monitors. The finish of that game is legend now.

Perkins is as relaxed on this show as Hergert has ever seen him. After Alabama is short on an attempted two-point conversion, he says, "We put that in there so some of our fans would know that we do have a two-point play."

At another point, when Bo Jackson breaks one of his better runs of the day—and he never got off the game breaker everyone expected—Perkins says, with his voice full of admiration, "You know, Dennis, I'd like to be that man's agent."

After the show, he lingers in the studio long enough to watch a recruiting tape that Hergert has put together for him. Perkins, along with some of the great names in Alabama football, will look into the camera and tell the high school players who watch the tape just how much it could mean to them to come to school here and be a part of the great tradition. Lee Roy speaks his piece, distinguished and graying, like the Dallas businessman he is. It is a long road from Excel.

Joe Namath remembers how "Football meant a lot to us in Alabama during some pretty rough times." Those were the civil rights years. It is clear that those days are gone by the number of black players featured on this tape. Walter Lewis, Jon Hand, Sylvester Croom who is now one of Perkins's assistants. All black.

Perkins announces that he is satisfied with the tape.

He drives to the athletic dormitory where he will eat breakfast with his wife and several recruits. There are also two friends who have come down to stay with the Perkinses for the weekend. A man he met while he was coaching at New England and a nun, Sister Carol Ann, who was a fierce Giants fan. Perkins made her an honorary coach of the team and she put on inspirational performances and did magic tricks for the players. She does a couple of those things this morning for these recruits.

The mood at breakfast is almost giddy. Laughter followed by long silences. Then, someone will remember another moment or another play from the game.

"When I saw Jelks slide through the hole and hit daylight, I just *knew*."

"Yes sir. Nobody was going to catch *him*. The kid can fly."

"And only a freshman."

"Outran Bo."

"Yeah. He sure did. But did you hear that Bo had two broken ribs?"

"Didn't play like it."

"No sir. He's all man."

After breakfast, Perkins takes each of the recruits aside for a private talk. One of them comes out of the room, after talking with Perkins, with something close to glee in his face. It looks like the boy is doing everything he can to keep from smiling or from just throwing his head back and howling with delight.

Then, with breakfast finished and the recruits each spoken to, Perkins gives his wife a kiss and climbs into his Lincoln for a drive out into the country to the farm he bought almost twenty years ago with his signing bonus, the first real money he'd ever seen in his life. He invites the visitor along.

Outside of Tuscaloosa, they stop at a little country store and buy some tobacco. And some cups to spit in. Then they are sliding along the greasy looking blacktop, through a cold, steady rain, chewing, spitting, and talking football. The visitor wonders just how much some Alabama fans would give to be sitting where he is right now.

But getting Perkins alone does not mean that he will suddenly open up and say things privately that he would not otherwise say. When the visitor asks him about Vince Sutton, the highly recruited quarterback who now sits on his bench, Perkins says just about what he said two weeks earlier in front of the Birmingham Quarterback Club.

"So far, Sutton has not been mentally tough enough to start at quarterback. And he's not a good enough athlete to play any other position. It's not a matter of ability. Mike Shula has average ability. But he is a competitor."

After last night and what Shula was able to do with fifty-seven seconds left in the most important game of his life, there is no arguing that.

Perkins and his visitor talk about some of the troubles. Does he think they are all behind him?

"No. Some people will be comparing me to Coach Bryant if I'm still here fifteen years from now. But that's all right. I'll still be doing things my way. I knew what to expect."

They drive by a large impoundment where two men in a bass boat are anchored and fishing in spite of the rain. Past prairies grown over in tawny colored broom weed. Past pine trees planted in regimentally straight rows.

Was there anything that was especially tough during those early days, the visitor asks. Anything that struck him as especially unfair.

"I kind of thought everyone would understand I'd want my own people."

Yes, the visitor says. He's read where that had been a consideration of Bryant's. He'd made sure that he had his own assistants and that the university would take care of the old ones, especially those like Hank Crisp who had been around a long time.

"Well, when I told him I would keep some of the defensive people but I'd have to let the offensive people go, he said, 'Well, you'll have to tell them.' "

This is said in a tone more of fatalism than bitterness. Perkins has been overcoming obstacles so long now, he expects them. And, say some, he actually welcomes them.

But this morning he is relaxed. He is proud of the farm with its new stables, and especially proud of the Arabian in one of them. It is a beautiful horse. A young animal with pads of muscle bunched under its carefully groomed coat. Perkins and his visitor lean over a wall, admiring the animal in silence.

He shows the visitor the little abandoned church and graveyard which he agreed to keep up in order to extend his property lines. Talks about the pond he wants to build. He is plainly attached to this place.

"Last year, when things were going so bad, I used to just get in the car and come out here for an hour. To get away from things. It would always clear my mind."

It is mid-morning when he starts back for town. He is flying to Fort Lauderdale in a couple of hours. Recruiting. He needs to see his wife and his guests before he leaves.

The visitor thanks him and Perkins shakes his hand and says, "I enjoyed it. And I'm glad you could see *that* game. Come back to Alabama again some time."

At about the time Perkins is taking off in the corporate jet owned by the athletic department, Pat Dye's show is on the television. The cameras do not go into the locker room, as they usally do, when the team leaves the field. Dye's first words to his team remain between him and them.

Dye is disappointed and subdued as he talks about the game. "We thought we had it won," he says. "If the ball carrier had stayed in bounds, there, on the play where they called the penalty, then that would have been it. We'd have scored and run the clock out." He also says that he thinks an Alabama fumble that was blown dead early in the game might have been crucial. But he doesn't say any of this with much conviction. He is too much what he is to make excuses. Auburn lost the game. There isn't anything else to say. So he soldiers through the replays. Thanks everyone who contributed to the season, including the band, and generally lets his co-host, Phil Snow, carry the show.

Later in the program, there are some interviews with weeping players in the dressing room. Snow says that he likes to talk to the Christian boys after a tough loss because they have something to say. The first player he talks to says, between sobs, that the Lord has a purpose to everything and maybe, in later years, he'll be able to understand what the Lord's purpose was tonight.

An Auburn fan watching the show says he thinks there are too many Christians on the team. "We need more SOBs," he says, "and fewer of those fellowship boys. There is a time for everything under the sun and when you play Alabama, it is a time to kick ass."

Bo Jackson says he thinks the team that played the hardest won. Jackson will win the Heisman, by the closest vote ever.

Alabama will go to Hawaii and win. Auburn will go to Dallas and lose. Perkins's contract will be extended. Dye, under rising pressure, will fire Jack Crowe and another assistant, named Frank Orgel. Dye and Orgel had been teammates and roommates once. Dye will also bring Pat Sullivan back to Auburn as an assistant coach. Both schools will claim success in the recruiting of high school ball players. Alabama fans will have a year of glory. Then, it will be November . . . and time to do it all again.